STAR TURNS

STAR TURNS

The Life and Times
of Benny Hill and Frankie Howerd

BARRY TOOK

WEIDENFELD & NICOLSON
London

First published in Great Britain in 1992 by
George Weidenfeld & Nicolson Limited
The Orion Publishing Group
Orion House,
5 Upper St Martin's Lane, London, WC2H 9EA

A catalogue reference is available from the British Library

ISBN 0 297 81297 1

Filmset by Selwood Systems, Midsomer Norton
Printed in Great Britain by
Butler & Tanner Ltd, Frome and London

Contents

Introduction

*M*y main problem in writing this book has not been what to put in but what to leave out.

I have talked to almost everyone who knew Benny Hill and Frankie Howerd; their agents, employers, scriptwriters, journalists, friends and enemies. I've heard them both called "mediocre" by some members of the theatrical profession, and "brilliant" by many others.

When I began I thought I knew Frankie Howerd well and Benny Hill hardly at all. Later I learned so much I hadn't known about Howerd that I realised I hardly knew him and was told so many contradictory stories about Benny Hill that I had to revise my views about them both and start again from scratch, as if both men were complete strangers to me.

To give some idea of the breadth of my enquiries, in the course of research I have spoken to or been in touch with Rupert Murdoch; David Attenborough; Roger Hancock (brother of Tony Hancock); Shaun Usher, senior feature writer of the *Daily Mail*; Ray Alan (but not Lord Charles!); the former controllers of BBC1 and BBC2, Paul Fox and Robin Scott; scriptwriters Ray Galton and Alan Simpson; Eric Sykes; Johnny Speight; former Head of Light Entertainment at Thames Television, Philip Jones (for whom Benny Hill worked for eighteen years); and his successor (the man who sacked Hill), John Howard Davies. I have watched dozens of videos and listened to a score of sound tapes and gramophone records.

One thing I have learned: individual memories are almost always inaccurate but fortunately the BBC's Written Archives centre at Caversham, and its helpful staff (they even offer tea and coffee at mid-morning and mid-afternoon to the weary researcher), has unearthed written evidence in the form of yellowing letters and inter-departmental memos, and correspondence with artists and agents, which have clarified otherwise obscure situations and have given me a clear picture of the events surrounding the careers of Benny Hill and Frankie Howerd.

Benny Hill: on the threshold of a remarkable career

By sad coincidence both men died within hours of each other on 19 April 1992, and I didn't know as I read Frankie Howerd's obituaries on that Monday morning, 20 April 1992, that during the past forty-eight hours (nobody was sure when) Benny Hill had also died, not as Frankie Howerd did – surrounded by his loved ones – but much as he had lived – alone.

David Wigg, in the *Daily Express*, wrote:

> Frankie's secret was that he could communicate with anyone and any age from Royalty to people with as humble an upbringing as himself...

and added a quote from Howerd:

> I work all the time but it's not for the cash... I love working.
> I do it for the challenge.

Steven Dixon of *The Guardian*, in his obituary of Frankie Howerd, said, "As a man he was a mass of complementary but usually conflicting neuroses." Howerd himself had said, "I was over-sensitive and frightened of failure ... but ... I learned the hard way. I learned through failure."

"High camp," said Adam Benedick in *The Independent*, and he was about right. Admittedly in most other respects he was wrong, getting Howerd's birthdate and birthplace wrong, not to mention the dates of his early career, but a hurried obituary of someone unknown to you is liable to error, although one mistake was understandable. Howerd had given his date of birth in *Who's Who* as 6 March 1922, and it was only recently that I found that Frankie Howerd was five years older than he ever admitted.

There was no mystery about Benny Hill's birthday (25 January 1924) although the rest of his life was something of a closed book.

Over the years I met Benny Hill on various occasions, and in the 1970s had interviewed him for a radio series I was making at the time, called *The Best of British Laughs*. I found him likeable and personally charming and, in his early BBC television shows, inventive and funny, but in his later work there were elements that I didn't like at all.

It seemed to me that a great deal of his material derived from other sources, and consciously or otherwise he had taken a number of ideas from other programmes and reworked them. There is no obvious harm in that because his versions of, for instance, the Rowan and Martin's *Laugh-In* "joke wall", or sketches on similar subjects to those tackled by other writers in other TV shows, were different in detail.

The problem for Benny Hill, as I saw it, was that he himself had dried up

"I was amazed!"

as a creative writer and was either reworking his own material or that of other people. The arrival of the brilliant troupe of dancers, Hill's Angels, helped lift his shows for a while but the repetition of western sketches and gangster sketches, the all too frequent use of "drag" where a dress, female make-up and a wig partly disguised the paucity of the dialogue, I found rather tedious.

He was not helped either, in my view, by his ageing male supporting cast who, with the honourable exception of Bob Todd, were not in the same class as the supporting company of Frankie Howerd's or Tony Hancock's shows, when actors of the calibre of Sid James, Kenneth Williams, Bill Kerr and Hattie Jacques helped to stimulate the star and add quality to the production.

Dave Freeman, a writer of great experience, worked with Benny Hill for ten years or so, but after he stopped, if other writers did contribute to the Benny Hill shows they were not credited.

Time and again as I watched the start of a sketch or routine my expectations would grow that maybe at last the old Benny Hill magic would work, but time and again my hopes were dashed as ragged continuity and hackneyed "business" with pawnbroker's signs, false teeth and the all but inevitable smart blow with pole, paddle or shaft between Hill's legs, made me long for the ordeal of watching the show to end. Frequently the battle against switching off was lost and I may have missed the strokes of genius that made Hill better known worldwide than Chaplin.

In the summer of 1992 while in France on holiday I watched a Benny Hill show on the French Channel 3. It was interesting to see what was on offer. The end credits stated that the show had been made in 1986, but it looked to me very much like a paste-up.

It started with a long sequence of sight gags concerning the adventures of a bucket. Then came Benny Hill, plump, well-dressed and charming, talking to the audience. This had been dubbed into French (possibly by Benny himself) and consisted mainly of him denying that he was sexist, with quips along the lines of "You never hear of a female chauvinist pig", which in translation didn't seem terribly funny, but was coupled with a deafening laughter track added afterwards by the engineers.

The show, which ran about twenty-four minutes, ended with Benny as a shortsighted handyman in a girls' school – the jokes mainly silent, often funny, accompanied by the inevitable rooty-toot-toot music – and concluded with him being chased by a crowd of schoolgirls, plus Bob Todd dressed as a woman.

An undemanding melange of mainly slapstick humour and in many ways better in the short version than in the longer editions seen in England. But with both Hill and Howerd on my mind how I longed for a touch of vintage Howerd, such as when he was called up for the army in 1940: "I hoped to be rejected on the grounds of insanity – no such luck" and, describing how he liked to walk whenever he had to learn lines, preferably in open spaces like fields, graveyards and parks, and on one such occasion while crossing a park mumbling his routine to himself, a young man called out, "Stop talking to yourself, it's the first sign of madness."

This jogged another memory of Benny Hill, also in a park, strolling with a young lady and being shouted at by a bunch of yobs, "You're nothing but a dirty old man", and Hill shouting back: "No I'm not. I'm a rich and famous dirty old man."

Howerd, though not averse to the company of young women, made much in his routines of his liking for the larger models. "I like them fat – there's more to choose from", and "Ooh, she was big. Every time she laughed everything quivered. It took an hour for it to settle", and "I prefer older women, they're more grateful."

That two men, who had between them nearly a hundred years of making people laugh, should die within hours of each other was sad and each will be missed.

Michael Billington, writing about Howerd and Hill in *The Guardian*, quoted Leigh Hunt:

> The death of a comic actor is felt more than that of a tragedian. He has sympathised more with us in our everyday feelings and has given us more amusement.

Few men in their lifetimes can have given more amusement than Frankie Howerd and Benny Hill.

1 *Growing up*

Should we be surprised that so many comedians have such similar emotional backgrounds? When asked about their childhood they talk of feelings of inadequacy, the desire to be noticed and to be special; the realisation, unconscious or not, that laughter is a weapon that can make up for any imagined lack of strength or academic ability.

The phrase "helpless with laughter" is one that comes to mind. There is no doubt that if you can immobilise your enemies or rivals by making them laugh you become at once the stronger party, and, of course, raising a laugh is extremely gratifying because the person raising the laugh is the centre of attraction and is, at least for the moment, admired.

However, many children feel inadequate but don't become comedians so there must be other elements at work. Let us look at our two star turns and see what we find.

Benny Hill

Benny Hill was born in Southampton on 25 January 1924 and christened Alfred Hawthorne Hill. He was preceded by a brother, Leonard, born in 1921, a sickly baby who grew into a sturdy, scholarly lad. Having tried his hand at entertaining, he forsook the make-up box for the blackboard jungle and became, in due course, a schoolmaster. He died of a heart attack in 1990.

A third child, a daughter, Diana, was born in 1933, grew up a warm and caring person, became a nurse, emigrated to Australia, but sadly died of leukaemia in 1987.

The Hill children's parents, Alfred and Helen, were quite different from each other. They had met and married in 1920 and settled in Helen's home town, Southampton. She was a homebody, an uncomplicated loving person who gave her children warmth, comfort and encouragement.

Hill senior was known as "the Captain" although he had served as a private

Alfred and Helen Hill, Benny's parents with
the "pretty baby"

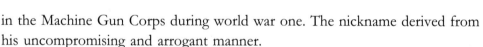

in the Machine Gun Corps during world war one. The nickname derived from his uncompromising and arrogant manner.

He had led something of a vagabond life before his army career, moving from job to job and even spending some time working in a circus. From all accounts his attitude towards authority of any kind was at best suspicious and generally deeply antagonistic, a state of mind common among those who had fought and suffered in "the Great War". He heartily agreed with the German general who described the British Army as "lions led by donkeys", and having served on the killing fields of the western front, been captured in an enemy attack, and spent time as a prisoner-of-war, he had little praise for the High Command.

Peace and repatriation did not soften his attitude and his son Leonard, in his book about his brother, *Saucy Boy*, paints a picture of a bullying martinet constantly having to prove to his sons how much stronger, cleverer, and more able he was.

In the case of Leonard that was not too difficult: "I was so ugly and sickly I startled visitors into frankness." His mother's sister, Louise, said, "Couldn't you do better than that?"

Two years later they produced Alfred junior (Benny) who was pretty and whose arrival cured the post-natal depression that had followed the arrival of Leonard and caused their mother such distress. It is here that we can catch a glimpse of the Benny Hill to come. Much loved and petted by his mother – "I think she was intoxicated by her love and her power over us," said Leonard – he returned that affection fully, even to the extent, when out walking, of holding her hand and rubbing his face in her fur cuff, crooning "lovely Mummy" the while.

In later life his genial, even loving, behaviour has been remarked upon by colleagues, both male and female.

Music came into the Hill household early as sailors arriving in Southampton from New York would bring the latest gramophone records of Fanny Brice, Whispering Jack Smith, and the Two Black Crows to the surgical appliance shop of which Benny Hill's father was the manager, and they would duly be played on the Hills' wind-up gramophone. The Captain also played the one-string fiddle while little Alfie sang.

Both brothers were expected to entertain, but only Benny really enjoyed it, re-telling jokes his mother read to him from comics and getting cross when he didn't receive everyone's complete attention.

As they grew older the Captain tried and failed to teach his sons to swim and to ride bicycles, his manner clearly inhibiting them. He gave them tasks around the house, but Benny adopted an attitude of assumed stupidity. It was "his first ploy in the struggle to resolve his relationship with his father, to deal with oppressive paternal domination", said Leonard.

His father responded, "Give it here. You've got no bloody idea, you bloody idiot." The contrast between the sweet, cuddling mother and the harsh, over-bearing father, with the child on one hand wanting to be the centre of attraction and indeed encouraged to be so, but on the other treated with scorn and contempt, meant that Benny Hill's childhood was fraught and difficult. Only when Benny became a star did his father grudgingly admit there was something in the boy.

The surgical appliance shop at which Hill senior worked was a back-street emporium dealing in various kinds of abdominal supports and obscure medicines designed to promote vigour. But the main business of the shop was supplying contraceptives either to customers in person or by post, doubtless "in a plain wrapper". It was an extremely successful business – the owner, Jack Stanley, became a millionaire – but Hill senior, unable to buy the partnership offered to him in 1920, remained an employee for the rest of his life, another source of bitterness.

It is said that at school young Benny was taunted with cries of "Hillie's dad sells french letters", another source of humiliation but one which gave him a chance to retaliate by using his assumed knowledge of sex to regale his fellow ragamuffins with schoolboy smut, a trait that never left him. One example, quoted by his brother Leonard, was in part justified in that it was a pun on a local beauty spot:

> *Teacher (to latecomer)*: Where have you been?
> *Schoolboy*: Up Shirley Hill.
> *Teacher (to late arriving schoolgirl)*: Who are you?
> *Schoolgirl*: I'm Shirley Hill.

At home he had to tread more carefully but he became adept at home entertainment, and in later years, appearing on *Desert Island Discs*, Benny remembered entertaining his family with impersonations of BBC radio stars of the day such as Claud Dampier, Horace Kenny, and Stainless Steven. Those were the days when Sir John (later Lord) Reith, the man who ran the BBC, decreed that "nothing should be broadcast which would bring a blush to a maiden's cheek", but Benny really preferred saltier material and when asked about his earlier amateur and semi-professional appearances, he answered Roy Plomley's question, "What act did you do?" by saying, "Anybody's, but largely Max Miller's."

Max Miller was the first and most famous of the overtly sexy comedians whose opening line in his act was frequently, "I'm filthy with money [pause] I'm filthy without it", and whose ploy of offering his audience a choice of two books of jokes: the white book "which has all the clean stories in it", and the blue book, "with all the others", guaranteed the audience baying for "the blue book, Max, the *blue* book". This must have impressed the teenage Benny Hill and given him an early insight into what audiences really wanted. Frankie Howerd, too, was greatly influenced by Max Miller, who was neither Liver-pudlian (like Arthur Askey and Ted Ray) nor American, but quintessentially English, and southern English at that, and something of a maverick. His outrageous clothes and swaggering "I don't care" attitude was a model for many young comedians of the day, much as a later crop have admired and imitated Ben Elton. Miller's greatest achievement was to draw his audience into a sort of conspiracy where secrets could be publicly shared, and both Hill and Howerd used this technique in their own performances.

By now determined that one day he would be an entertainer, Hill fell behind in his school work, being interested in French but otherwise no scholar. The early teens are a trying time for many people, but Benny, in spite of being able to make his family and school friends laugh, seems, like so many other comedians, to have felt deeply insecure.

According to his brother Leonard, he was full of "psychological tension", compulsively biting his nails to the quick and going for long, lonely walks. Sometimes these walks had an object in view. Benny recounted one such walk to Roy Plomley.

"It was my first-ever romance. The biggest I've ever had. I was twelve, she was fourteen, and I saw this lovely girl with dark brown hair, dressed in a green coat." It was during a September Carnival Week and Benny was staying with his cousin in Eastleigh, some six miles from his Southampton home. "I fell like mad for this girl and found out where she lived." According to his cousin, the girl used to take lunch into her father's shop in Market Street, Eastleigh every day. So, when Christmas came – "The very first day of the holiday I said to my mother, 'I think I'll go out for a walk.'" And walk he did, the six miles to Eastleigh. "I stood at the end of Market Street, watched her go into the shop with her father's lunch – and come out of the shop with the empties. That was my day made. I did it day after day all through the holidays, six miles there and back, rain, hail, sleet or snow." And he never spoke to her! At the end of the holidays he went back to school and forgot all about her. Benny added laconically, "I think my dad bought me a football."

I feel that the story of Benny's unrequited love for the dark-haired girl in the green coat, apart from being quite romantic, is symbolic of his attitude to the opposite sex in later life. Whatever his attitude to women on the screen, who were portrayed as nubile nymphets, embittered nagging harridans, or vampires, I have never heard from any of the many people I have talked to about Benny Hill anything to his discredit regarding his behaviour with women. He appears to have been gentle, gallant and courteous throughout his life.

Not so to his father. Hill revenged himself by mocking him and turning their relationship into a series of comic playlets in which the father was portrayed as a gangster. However jokey these episodes must have seemed, deep down Benny felt a great deal of hatred for his father, confiding to his brother

Leonard when they were much older, "There were times when I could have cheerfully killed him."

Benny left school early and had various menial daytime jobs including working in the stockroom of a Woolworth's store and as a milkman, which he clearly enjoyed and which many years later inspired his best-selling record "Ernie, The Fastest Milkman in the West".

During this period of his life he also flourished as a semi-professional entertainer playing drums and guitar, singing and cracking jokes. So popular was he that one concert secretary said to him as he paid him his fee, "Sorry it's only five shillings. You're worth every penny of seven and sixpence."

So in his determination to become a professional entertainer in 1941, at the age of seventeen, he left Southampton for London and showbiz.

Frankie Howerd

Frankie Howerd was born in York and christened Francis Alick Howard, not in 1922 as he later related, but on 6 March 1917, which made him seventy-five and not seventy when he died.

His father, Francis Alfred William Howard, was a regular soldier. In his autobiography, *On The Way I Lost It*, Howerd described him as a sergeant in the Royal Artillery. Again Howerd was less than accurate. According to the birth certificate which I found in St Catherine's House he was a private (No. 6759) in the 1st Royal Dragoons. His mother, Edith Florence, née Morrison,

"Not a titter" –
unsmiling Frankie with his mother

came from Scotland and was working in York when she met and married the handsome dragoon. When Frankie was nearly three his father was posted to Woolwich Barracks and the family set up home in Eltham, coincidentally the birthplace in 1903 of another famous comedian, Bob Hope.

The Howard family grew with the birth of another son, Sidney, and five years later a daughter, Bettina, known as Betty.

From all accounts Frank Howard senior was a dour man who suffered from ill-health. After a spell in the Army Education Corps, where his duties took him all over the country, he was finally invalided out of the service and died when Frankie was in his teens.

In fact Frankie saw little of his father who, when he was at home, seemed an intruder on the warm relationship his children had with their cheerful mother with her "way out" sense of humour and her love of the theatre. It was Edith who gave Frankie his first taste of theatre, the pantomime at the Woolwich Artillery Theatre.

The Howard family was not well off and the theatre visits were rare treats, but Frankie and a small girl from next door, Ivy Smith, made up for that by staging home-made entertainments in their back garden, and charging the local children a farthing admission fee.

When his mother found out she was horrified and made them give the money back. She reprimanded Frankie by saying, "How dare you *rob* these children." Frankie himself commented in his autobiography, "I was affronted even at that early age for I assumed that if I charged a farthing and kids paid I just had to be worth it."

Although this paints a picture of Howerd as an entrepreneur he was in fact a lonely and introspective youth. Unlike Benny Hill, whose family were stoutly agnostic, Frankie found consolation and fellowship in religion and in particular the Sunday School at the Church of St Barnabas where he felt secure and, in his own words, "became extremely religious going on to join the Band of Hope, the Cubs, the Society for the Propagation of the Gospel. I joined everything religious in sight."

His mother with her Scottish Presbyterian background was delighted and had hopes that one day her boy Francis would view the Church as a vocation and become a clergyman. Frankie's aspirations were higher. He said, "I decided to become a saint."

For those of us who knew him in later life that is a grade one eyebrow raiser, for whatever Frankie Howerd was, a saint he was not.

However, in his young days this lonely, shy youth must have felt that Heaven was infinitely preferable to the poverty and drabness of life in Eltham. By hard work and effort Frankie won a scholarship to Shooters Hill Grammar School where his best subject was maths. He was also good if erratic as a cricketer, once getting six wickets in six balls, but on a bad day liable to bowl "wide enough to break a pavilion window".

At thirteen he became a Sunday School teacher spicing the Biblical stories

Frankie as a young man [standing] with brother Sidney and sister Betty

with inventions of his own and often adding tales of Robin Hood and other folk heroes to his repertoire. Unsurprisingly he was one of the most popular teachers.

His involvement in church matters led to his joining the Church Dramatic Society and playing the part of Tilly's father in Ian Hay's old comedy, *Tilly of Bloomsbury*. At the audition he stammered and stuttered and seemed hopeless in the part, but the producer, Winifred Young, took him in hand and her twice-weekly lessons helped Frank to master his stutter and assisted him in gaining a stage presence. In short, he was a smash hit in *Tilly of Bloomsbury* and got a good write-up in the local paper. He later admitted, "I owe as much to Winifred Young as to anyone else in my career."

After the performance one of the people backstage uttered the immortal words, "You should be an actor", and for young Francis Howard the die was cast; the shy, stuttering introvert had one goal in life – to be a professional actor. He blossomed in the school dramatic society and later, when he was sixteen, he enrolled for evening classes in acting promoted by the London County Council. One of the teachers was the actress Mary Hope, who saw in the youngster a gleam of talent. She coached him for an audition at RADA (Royal Academy of Dramatic Art) which, had he passed, would have secured him a scholarship and a chance to learn at one of the world's best drama schools.

Alas, by the time he arrived for the audition he was a bag of nerves, his speech impediment returned fourfold as, clutching a packet of cheese sandwiches which his mother had thoughtfully provided for his lunch, he stumbled incompetently through the set pieces, made a hash of the *Hamlet* soliloquy, and was duly failed. Looking back, it was probably a good day for British comedy. While we have many fine actors in Britain, truly great comedians are as rare as hen's teeth – and Frankie Howerd at his best was a great comedian.

His family made sacrifices to send him to grammar school, and to back his theatrical aspirations. Sidney and Betty both left school at fourteen and went to work. With Frank senior in poor health and providing little money, Edith became housekeeper to a wealthy family in Eltham in order to boost the family income, and by so doing helped to sustain her eldest son's ambitions.

Somehow the family kept going and Frankie, now joined by his sister Betty, starred in a number of charity concerts, acting in sketches of his own devising. He also rejoined the Church Dramatic Society and the Shooters Hill Old Boys Dramatic Society, but with school and the RADA debacle behind him Frankie realised that if he was not to be a great straight actor then he must turn his attention to comedy.

Like Benny Hill, Frank took undemanding, boring clerical jobs during the day and spent his evenings and weekends writing and devising entertainments. There was one proviso: he had to be the star. One of his efforts was called the Gertchers Concert Party, and another Frank Howard's Knock Out Concert Party, in which he was in twenty-one of the twenty-two items.

This suggests a blossoming ego and a self-confidence at odds with his earlier shyness. I suppose the root was sensitivity plus something that would be there throughout Frankie Howerd's life, the ability to overcome disaster and fight back. His professional career would prove a switchback: enormous success followed by troughs of indifference from both bookers and audiences, then by more success.

Profoundly depressed by the failure of his audition for RADA, he tended to react dramatically to the setbacks which were inevitable in the career of any aspiring performer. But he learned to overcome depression, helped in no small measure by his mother and his sister Betty.

One odd hiccup in the aspiring comedian's pre-war career was the curious decision to re-christen himself Ronnie Ordex, a name which sounds more like a brand of eyewash than a stand-up comedian. However this aberration was short-lived and he soon reverted to his given name.

From concert parties he graduated to talent nights at the neighbourhood music halls where, each Friday, local turns were encouraged to have a go. Frank Howard was a constant contributor, and a constant failure. On one occasion, at the Lewisham Hippodrome, he finished up tongue-tied and unable to speak while the musical director hissed, "Do something or get off." Frankie confessed, "I stumbled off in tears."

All these disasters and disappointments were actually to benefit him in the long run, because when he did get it right he was a sensational success. But first there was a war to be fought.

2 *At war with the army*

War, as we all know, consists of long periods of boredom interspersed with short periods of intense fear and danger, but in those long periods of inaction anyone with any skill at entertaining is a godsend, and Benny Hill and Frankie Howerd were part of the great wave of talent generated by world war two.

The professional organisation, a department of the NAAFI, responsible for entertainment to the forces in wartime was known by its acronym ENSA, which stood for Entertainment National Services Association, or as it was soon christened by the troops, "Every Night Something Awful". The fare consisted initially of old music hall and pierrot show entertainers pulled out of retirement and sent off to anti-aircraft batteries, army camps, naval depots and the like to give of their best to the young servicemen. Not all the ENSA entertainers were has-beens, however, and some famous names did their bit to entertain the troops, among them Noël Coward, Evelyn Laye, Roger Livesey, Ursula Jeans, Robert Newton, and Vera Lynn.

Soon after war was declared Frankie Howerd auditioned for ENSA, but was turned down. The following year – he had just turned twenty-three – he was called up, joined the Royal Artillery and was posted to Shoeburyness, where he acquired the nickname "the Unknown Quantity". After basic training he was moved to another part of the barracks where, mercifully for him, a YMCA staged Sunday night concerts.

As the leading light of these ad hoc entertainments he was introduced as Gunner *Frankie* Howard of B Battery. At first he didn't care for the name as he had never been called Frankie before, but the audience of young servicemen thought otherwise and "Frankie" he became once and for all. But he was still Howard.

After the invasion scare of summer 1940, when, according to Howerd, he was virtually the sole defender of Southend-on-Sea, he duly returned to the Shoeburyness barracks, where at those Sunday occasions at the YMCA he soon became wildly popular and always topped the bill.

As his skill and his ambitions grew, he developed what became the Howerd style during this period. It was a style, so he claimed, that was a mixture of a nervous stammer and a lack of good material. In short, he would take a well-worn joke and re-work it using the "oohs and aahs" and the "there was this woman", buttonholing his audience into a shared conspiracy in which the joke became incidental to the long and rambling story into which he turned it.

Admittedly his audiences were uncritical, but they were the first to taste the heady mixture of banter, insult and denigration that became Frankie Howerd's hallmark.

He developed other routines at this time, including a song which he did with two other soldiers dressed as ATS girls, Miss Twillow, Miss True, and Miss Twit. It was an easy act to get together when performed in barracks where any number of ATS girls of all shapes and sizes were stationed and uniforms were easy to come by.

However, Frankie and Co. were now also part of a civilian concert party called the Co-odments which toured the Southend area in an old van, entertaining the troops. Outside camp, ATS uniforms were harder to secure, but, by some shrewd flattery and even confidence trickery, they always found three suitable ATS girls prepared to lend theirs – in which they performed while the girls sat shivering in the dressing room.

Working with the Co-odments Frankie met two women who were to play a big part in his subsequent career, Vere Roper and Blanche Moore, each of whom became, in turn, his much-maligned, allegedly deaf accompanists of "poor soul, she's past it" fame.

"As you were!" In Ulster Frankie Howerd remembers his own army days

In due course Frankie was posted to Wales and thence to Plymouth in time for the 1944 Allied invasion of France.

Still trying to escape from normal military duties to the more comfortable world of entertaining, he recalled to Jack de Manio in a radio interview in 1976 that four times he auditioned for Stars In Battledress, the big army concert party, and failed each of them. The auditions were usually held in a cookhouse on a dark and rainy morning in front of one officer, but as his style required the intimate involvement of an audience these were hardly ideal circumstances. However, just after the war was over, by now promoted to sergeant and stationed in Germany, Frankie did get his wish, but owing to a shortage of talent his concert party became "almost a one-man show".

When another audition beckoned at Nienburg, he travelled with no expectation other than the by now inevitable rejection. But fortune at last smiled on Frankie. The officer in charge was Major Richard Stone (later Colonel Stone, and later still one of Britain's leading theatrical agents) who had before the war been an actor in a repertory company, and understood showbusiness. He liked Frankie's routine, as did his number two, Captain Ian Carmichael.

They put Sergeant Howard in charge of a concert party touring north-west Germany, but three months later, after six years in uniform, he was demobbed and became once again a civilian – "with less than £100, a chalk-striped suit, pork pie hat", and a kindly reference from his last army boss, Colonel Stone.

During his final months in the army he had met Benny Hill who was at that time mainly stage managing. Hill later recounted that he had enjoyed Howerd's performance, but that Frankie was gloomy about his future.

Here we can see a profound difference in the two men's attitudes to their careers; Howerd the eternal pessimist, Hill with an almost complete belief in his ultimate stardom.

Benny Hill, seven years younger than Howerd, had got himself a job as assistant stage manager of a touring revue by the simple act of calling at the stage door of the Chelsea Palace music hall in 1941 and asking if they needed a bright young entertainer. Well, it was wartime and, with so many men and women called up or directed to war work, there was an acute shortage of labour; Benny was taken on as ASM and general dogsbody.

He had been touring the smaller variety theatres for some months when, in Cardiff, two large policemen appeared at the stage door and arrested him as a deserter. In fact, touring as he had been, and moving week by week from town to town, his call-up papers had never reached him. He duly arrived at Catterick camp in Yorkshire under guard and became a private in the REME (Royal Electrical and Mechanical Engineers).

Officially he was described as a driver/mechanic, but he confessed to Roy Plomley, when appearing on *Desert Island Discs* in 1959, "I was the world's worst driver." After he was demobbed he never drove again. Nor did Howerd,

A serious young soldier

though taught to drive in the army. When I first met him, in 1955, he was driven everywhere by a lugubrious chauffeur, who doubled as his valet.

Hill confessed that he was a rotten soldier, but his cheerful disposition made him popular with his fellows. In France and Germany in 1944–5 he revealed a gift for languages and became fluent in both. His love of France and Germany developed in this period and would last all his life.

It was a time, too, when love of the human, not to say carnal side of life was revealed to the young soldier, although he would say later, "In relations between the sexes the male is always disappointed."

Meanwhile his theatrical ambitions didn't flourish when a humourless major, watching the dress rehearsal of a show in which Benny had the job of compère and occasional comedian, said in effect, "This man's not funny," and banished him. However, someone with more insight had been watching from the wings, and after the dress rehearsal this silent watcher introduced himself as Harry Segal and invited young Hill to the NAAFI for a cup of tea. In showbusiness since he was a child, Segal was now a sergeant running a touring revue called *It's All In Fun*. He felt the major was wrong about Benny's performance, but saw that poor Hill was shattered. In short, he took Benny with him as stage manager, assuring him that once away from HQ he would put him back on stage. Benny was reluctant to appear in public again, but bit by bit Harry Segal boosted his confidence, started using him in sketches and eventually insisted he did a five-minute stand-up solo spot. Benny demurred – "That's an order," said Sergeant Segal.

Benny, expecting the worst, went on, got laugh after laugh, and finished to a standing ovation. As luck would have it the same Colonel Stone who had rescued Frankie Howerd from oblivion was in the audience. "I thought he was wonderful," he recalled. Indeed, when the war was over and Richard Stone became a theatrical agent, Benny Hill was one of his first clients, another being the former Captain Ian Carmichael.

Benny Hill and Frankie Howerd were not the only comedians to benefit from the forcing house of wartime entertainment, and many of the post-war stars of radio, TV, stage and film went through the same baptism of theatrical fire and brought to peacetime comedy a freshness and style never before equalled.

The list is long: Tony Hancock, Peter Sellers, Dick Emery, Jimmy Edwards, Sid Colin, Kenneth Horne, Richard Murdoch, Frank Muir and Denis Norden served in the RAF. Charlie Chester, Harry Secombe, Arthur Haynes, Spike Milligan, Norman Vaughan, and Kenneth Williams were in the Army, Jon Pertwee and Eric Barker in the Navy, and there are many more performers, writers, and radio and TV producers who served their country in war and were determined that in peace they would make their mark. I think it is true to say that no men made their mark more indelibly than Benny and Frankie.

But there *is* a funny side to army life

3 *Peacetime*

Their army experiences had given Benny Hill and Frankie Howerd the conviction that there was a pot of gold at the end of the show-business rainbow, but they were not alone.

In the months after demobilisation all these emerging comedians found that no agent would book them until he had seen them perform, but without a booking they couldn't be seen. After tramping round agents' offices in his new civvy suit without success, Frankie Howerd, remembering his triumph in uniform, put on his khaki battledress again and turned up at the Stage Door Canteen, a haven for servicemen in London's Piccadilly Circus. Some of the greatest international stars, including Bob Hope and Bing Crosby, had played there during and immediately after the war, but the "bread and butter" entertainment was provided by returned ex-servicemen and a sprinkling of civilian entertainers.

Since he was no longer a soldier Frankie Howerd wasn't really entitled to wear uniform, but by so doing he wangled the chance to perform in front of an all-forces audience and having so wangled he invited an agent, Harry Lowe, to see him work.

Alas, although Frankie triumphed Harry Lowe didn't show. Bitter dis-appointment! But the Stage Door Canteen had a vacant spot the following Friday. Would "Sergeant" Howerd like to fill it? Well, he thought, what's the point, but encouraged by his mother he decided that perhaps he would have a go after all. He duly appeared and was again triumphant and this time, by some trick of fate, a variety agent *was* in the audience. Curiously, in his autobiography Howerd didn't mention the name of this good fairy, but he was Stanley Dale, known as "Scruffy", a booker working for Jack Payne. Payne had been a highly successful bandleader, but was now a theatrical agent and impresario. Stanley Dale had been invalided out of the RAF and had joined Payne in a fairly menial position.

Through Dale's recommendation Howerd duly met a senior member of the

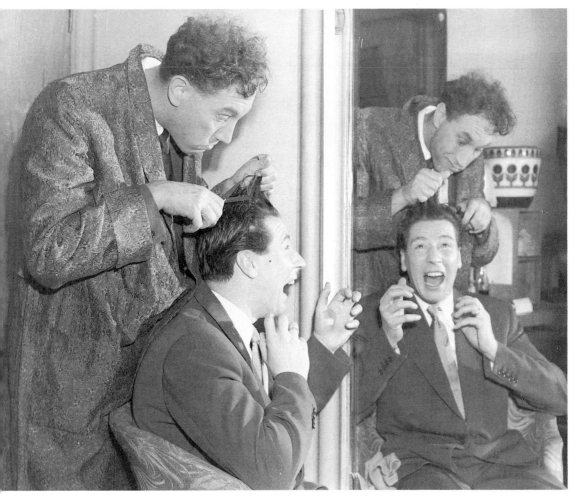

"*No* Frankie, I don't *want* hair like yours." Frankie Howerd and Max Bygraves

Payne organisation, Frank Barnard, and after a thundering row because, it seems, of Barnard's insufferable rudeness, Frankie Howerd auditioned "cold" (that's to say alone in the man's office) and Barnard, clearly a man of wild swings of emotion, thought him hilarious. In due course the great Jack Payne also saw Howerd stealing the show at a troop concert and booked him in a touring revue, *For The Fun Of It*. It was at this time that Frank Howard, having accepted that he was now Frankie, decided to adapt his surname to Howerd "to make it look different", and Frankie Howerd he stayed for the rest of his life.

The headliner of *For The Fun Of It* was the singer Donald Peers, then at the zenith of his career, and the newly-minted Frankie Howerd shared bottom of the bill, in a feature called "They're Out", with another up-and-coming comedian, Max Bygraves.

When the show opened in Sheffield in the summer of 1946, both Howerd and Bygraves were tremendously successful, thanks to a combination of youth, the fact that they had been in the services, and the freshness of their material.

Frankie's act was a monologue and the song "Three Little Fishes", a number he had used in his act since his pre-war concert-party days.

If you have not been granted the strange experience of the Howerd rendition no explanation will really do it justice. It is, let's face it, a silly song. The lyrics are:

> Down in the meadow in an itty bitty pool
> Swam three little fishes and a mama fishie too
> Swim, said the mama fishie
> Swim if you can
> And they swam and they swam all over the dam
>
> CHORUS
> Boop boop dittem dottem whattem Chu!
> Boop boop dittum dottem whattem Chu!
> Boop boop dittem dottem whattem Chu!
> And they swam and they swam all over the dam

Frankie's method was to sing with gestures and at the end of a "boop boop" line he'd emit an ear-splitting "choo" that in fact sounded like a Strasbourg goose which has just heard the bad news about its liver.

In the second verse a shark comes into it somehow and then (after a pause for breath) the audience would be invited to join in and another chorus was sung with everyone letting out a variety of wild squawks. It sounds – and was – pretty basic stuff, but very effective.

However, playing to soldiers in YMCAs and NAAFI units is one thing and appearing in grand variety theatres quite another so a different technique had to be learned. His sister Betty proved invaluable. Now demobbed from the ATS, she toured with him and acted as his unofficial (unpaid) stage manager. She told BBC producer John Browell in an interview:

> Frank was always passionately interested in the theatre from being a small
> child and ... was always very conscious of his audience and that they
> could hear him and see him clearly.
>
> I had to go to all parts of the theatre to see if they could see and hear
> him. I'd start in the stalls then go up to the circle and then the gallery.
> If there were problems I would tell him and he would then alter things
> so everyone could see and hear his act.

In looks he appeared not to care. Apart from following Max Miller's example – lots of blue on his eyelids "to help the eyes sparkle" – he used little make-up and wore an ordinary lounge suit which he said was "far from immaculate". That I can believe as Frankie Howerd even at his smartest was a tailor's nightmare.

The whole point of his act was to look ordinary, as if he had just walked in off the street – in a word, untheatrical. In this in one town he succeeded only too well, the local theatre critic saying he was unprofessional. "This man wears no make-up, doesn't dress, doesn't even take a bow at the end."

The latter comment referred, I guess, to another element borrowed from Max Miller who used to say, apropos taking a bow, "What's the point of bobbing in and out all the time." Frankie wrote to the critic explaining why he did what he did: "... looking bewildered as though by the fact that people think me funny". The critic replied: "You certainly bewildered *me*, and I thought you were singularly unfunny."

The critic was in a minority because most people enjoyed this new style of stream-of-consciousness humour and Frankie went from strength to strength. In 1946 when he had been a fully-fledged professional for only six weeks, Stanley Dale contacted him with the news that Joy Russell Smith, the BBC's producer of *Variety Bandbox*, the top variety show of that period, was auditioning for a new regular act.

It was either a great compliment to Frankie or an astute move on the part of Stanley Dale which got him the audition, but he turned up in a still sandbagged audition studio in Broadcasting House, went through his routine, and Joy Russell Smith was delighted, describing his act as "an entirely new art form". The memo recording the event reads as follows:

FRANKIE HOWERD (auditioned 9.10.46)

c/o Scruffy Dale

Very funny, original patter and song.

Eric Spear and John Hooper present and agree. Seeded.

Joy Russell Smith

With that recommendation Frankie Howerd started a broadcasting career that lasted forty-five years.

On *Variety Bandbox* he alternated every other week with an already-established comedian, Derek Roy, and the difference in the two men's styles could not have been more marked. Derek Roy used wisecracks in the American manner: sharp, polished and almost completely artificial. Frankie Howerd was stumbling, anecdotal, and totally real.

His debut was on 3 December at the Camberwell Palace, a theatre adapted for the use of radio variety shows. My own memory of hearing Frankie Howerd for the first time, early in 1947, was that something wonderful had happened. Here was somebody new in comedy, with a fresh personality, who made the smart-aleck comedians look tawdry. I was in the RAF at the time and playing trumpet in one of the dance bands that most RAF stations boasted. My own

"Ladies and gentle*men*!"

taste in comedy was Richard Murdoch, and Kenneth Horne in radio's *Much Binding in the Marsh*, and on the stage the great Sid Field, and Sidney Howard (no relation), an old hand at revue with a manner of lugubrious solemnity which was highly diverting. On the music hall stage my absolute favourite was Jimmy James, whose routines and timing were sublime. But once heard Frankie Howerd became for me the one new comedian I had to listen to.

Unlike Hill and Howerd I had at that time no taste for performing, but had vague ambitions to be a technician in a film studio, or a dance band musician. Later in my RAF service I told some jokes at a concert and became as besotted with laughter-making as the heroes of this book, and make no mistake, although Hill and Howerd were each in their way deeply flawed men, in their chosen profession they did attain heroic stature.

It is hard to remember now the impact that Frankie Howerd made in his first broadcast in 1946. It was the rare case of someone becoming "a star overnight", but it had taken him over twenty years as an amateur and six months as a professional to do it.

By spring of 1947 Frankie Howerd had become one of the most popular entertainers in the business – and rich? No. Here's why.

In 1947 the Jack Payne Organisation put Frankie Howerd under a personal management contract, which meant that while he received a regular income Payne's company could pocket more than an agent's normal ten per cent and secure a larger rake-off if their management skills brought their artist more and better work.

The logistics were that if Frankie earned £100 a week he would receive £62.10 shillings and Payne would receive £37.10 shillings. Not totally unreasonable for a performer in his first year as a professional, and – with certain misgivings – Frankie Howerd duly signed up for five years.

With his success on radio he now became a big draw in the theatre, playing to full houses whether in a summer show, in music halls or in pantomime. He was (in theory) earning big money, but the ball and chain of the Payne contract meant that while he was doing well Jack Payne was making a small fortune.

For instance, in 1950 when he was starring at the London Palladium in a show called *Out Of This World*, he received a salary of £600 per week of which Payne took nearly £300. But Payne had also made a separate contract with the impresario, Val Parnell, whereby he received an extra £300 for Howerd's services.

Howerd objected, Payne claimed that it was compensation for sub-letting him to Parnell which prevented Payne using him in his own shows. It sounds pretty shabby, and in fact Howerd's legal advisers (not to mention Stanley Dale, who by now had left Payne) considered that by these actions Payne had broken his contract, which was now null and void.

Payne objected and the matter was finally resolved in the High Court in 1951. Howerd won, Payne's counter-claim was dismissed and he was ordered to pay Howerd the sum of £5,216. To Frankie Howerd it was not so much the money, but the fact that he was now free of Payne and could pursue his career more or less as he wished.

Throughout the dispute Howerd had been aided and abetted by Stanley Dale. Let us look at Frankie's career from 1946–51 from a fiscal point of view.

1946: Howerd's first fee was eighteen guineas per programme for *Variety Bandbox*.

1947: He received twenty-five guineas.

1949: The BBC were informed that in future all correspondence with Frankie Howerd should be sent to 6 Holland Villas Road, Frankie's London address. It was in fact a flat in a house owned by the comedian Ben Warris, which Frankie rented.

Later in 1949 Stanley Dale let it be known that he was now Frankie Howerd's personal manager, and he must have been good, because in 1950 Frankie's radio fee rose to £100 per programme.

In February 1951 letters to the BBC came from Frankie Howerd Ltd (Directors: F. Howerd, S. Dale, E. F. Howerd (Frankie's mother)), 130 Uxbridge Road, W12. On 22 February a further communication to the BBC came from Frankie Howerd Scripts Ltd (Directors: F. Howerd, S. Dale, E. Sykes), address, unsurprisingly, 130 Uxbridge Road, which consisted of two floors over a greengrocer's shop, converted to offices used by Eric Sykes, Spike Milligan, and later Ray Galton, Alan Simpson and others. Frankie Howerd Scripts Ltd. was the nucleus of what was to become one of the most powerful scriptwriters' and artists' agencies of the day – Associated London Scripts, whose directors included Howerd, Ray Galton and Alan Simpson, Tony Hancock, Spike Milligan and Eric Sykes, and whose clients included many of the best comedy writers around, including Johnny Speight (Arthur Haynes, *Till Death Us Do Part*), and Terry Nation (the man who invented the Daleks). The man who welded these components together was the enigmatic Stanley Dale.

No wonder he was known as "Scruffy" – he was terminally unkempt. He rarely got up before noon and would receive visitors while in bed in his pyjamas. It was rumoured that he had been an unsung hero in the war where his quickness of wits saved the aeroplane, and its crew, in which he was an air gunner. But nobody actually believed anything he said. He might have been a hero. On the other hand he may never have seen action. Nobody knew.

Stanley could however spot talent. His big find was a young comedian named Jim Smith. Stanley Dale immediately saw his star quality, put him under contract, continued to pay him during his RAF national service, and with the coming of the youth culture of the late 1950s early 1960s changed his name to Jim Dale and secured him major exposure in BBC TV's pop music show, *6.5 Special*. Jim Dale remembers Stanley Dale with a kind of amused tolerance:

> Oh, he was a good agent and got me a lot of work but he was always
> "doing deals". For instance, I wanted a car and he said, "Leave it to me,"
> so we went to this secondhand car showroom and he haggled with the

dealer and paid for the car in cash. I repaid him over the next few months (with added interest), but I think it would have cost me less to buy a new car myself.

The car, as I remember it, was a pink Vauxhall Cresta which, I suppose, fitted the image of an up-and-coming pop star in the late 1950s.

Stanley also persuaded Jim Dale to take out an insurance policy and Jim laughed as he told me, "I have a feeling that he was an agent for the insurance company and got a rake-off."

Personally, I owe Stanley Dale a lot, because although he had his peculiarities – as indeed it seemed did everybody in Associated London Scripts – he booked me on variety bills, persuaded the powerful Moss Empire chain to engage me, and even lent me the money to buy my first house.

For a time I shared an office in a house he owned, 12 Holland Villas Road, and although at the time I knew no more about him than I have written here, I don't think anyone else knew much more about him either.

Frankie Howerd, in his autobiography, never mentions what went wrong with their relationship, but like it or not Stanley Dale played a big part in the rise of Frankie Howerd and is to be remembered and thanked for that.

Much of this success was built on the skill of one man, Eric Sykes. It was Sykes' scripts when he became Howerd's regular writer in 1947 which confirmed Howerd as a genuine top-liner. Their wonderful storylines gave radio an element of surreal comedy not heard since Robb Wilton, such as the routine he wrote in which Frankie recounted his adventures taking two elephants to Crewe. Another, of which I only remember a fragment, concerned travelling from Manchester to London by air in a very old aeroplane. "It took ages to take off . . . in fact we went as far as Birmingham by road."

Sykes' great skill was to create pictures in the mind. As he matured and developed he became a key factor in the success of the radio series *Educating Archie*, and evolved his own starring performing style on TV in Val Parnell's *Saturday Spectacular* variety shows, and later in a long-running BBC sit. com. with Hattie Jacques, Deryck Guyler and Richard Wattis.

It was Sykes who wrote most of Frankie Howerd's scripts for *Variety Bandbox*, and when Howerd decided to quit the show in 1951 it was natural that Eric Sykes should write his next venture – another radio series, called *Fine Goings On*. For reasons hard to analyse now this new show, in spite of support from Hattie Jacques, didn't make much impact. Only one series was made and Howerd was at a loss as to what to do next.

It was his habit, acquired in his teens in Eltham, that when he had a problem he would go for long lonely walks during which he would think about the future and decide what to do next. A thought struck Howerd during one of these walks:

> Why not take a small unit and record a series of shows with the troops
> … and with the help of the BBC and the War Office I worked out an
> itinerary that would include Tripoli and Benghazi, Egypt, Jordan, Cyprus
> and Malta. In the party were singer Marcia Owen, pianist Blanchie Moore,
> and Eric Sykes to write the scripts.

The title of the series was *Frankie Howerd Goes East* and, apart from the professionals in the group, servicemen were recruited as ad hoc actors for the sketches. In addition to the series of programmes recorded for the BBC they gave concerts wherever troops, the RAF or the Navy were to be found.

These extensive tours were popular with the servicemen abroad as well as with listeners at home, but as a regular event in Frankie's life they came to an end in 1971 on a slightly sour note. At that time I was Head of Light Entertainment at London Weekend Television and looking around for something different to put on the screen. One day a public relations officer from the RAF came to see me and asked if there was any way LWT and the RAF could be of mutual help. I remembered Frankie's earlier successes doing troop shows and suggested that perhaps Frankie Howerd and a group of actors and singers touring the world's far-flung airbases might be something worth considering. The PRO jumped at the idea, and suggested that the RAF would provide all transport and accommodation and that LWT should provide the rest.

I then contacted Beryl Vertue, who at that time represented both Frankie Howerd and Galton and Simpson. She consulted them, they agreed, and we worked out a deal. While I discussed casting and sketch ideas with the principals concerned, the RAF flew my assistant, Mike Smith, and a senior LWT engineer to recce and report on all the bases at which we proposed to put on shows. The locations we had chosen were Gibraltar, Malta, Cyprus, Gan in the Indian Ocean (a refuelling airstrip), Hong Kong, and a base in Germany.

All was well under way when London Weekend suffered a minor earthquake in the shape of Rupert Murdoch, the then Australian newspaper proprietor. I say '*then*' Australian because since those days he has adopted American citizenship. Anyway, Murdoch had bought shares in LWT which were previously owned by Lord Weinstock of GEC and thought that by so doing he

"Hello sailor. New in Gib?"

had bought the company. He was later disabused and sold out, but for a time he roamed the offices of LWT telling us all how things should be done.

The truth was that he knew little of the problems of a British commercial television station and his advisers seemed to know less. On hearing of the Howerd project he went into tailspin, cancelled it, and said in effect: "I understand this man Howerd is a little effeminate. I can't have him roaming round the world with all those young servicemen." He didn't say this to me, incidentally, but it was a decision that seemed a little naive coming from a man who owned and promoted the style of his newspapers, the *Sun* and the *News of the World.*

Years after the event and with its principal victim in his grave, it still annoys me that something as simple, effective, and potentially popular – not to say incredibly inexpensive – should have been stopped on such insubstantial grounds. Perhaps Rupert Murdoch was right, but in 1971 it didn't seem so to me.

In 1991, in one of the last shows he ever recorded, Frankie Howerd again played to a service audience, the crew of HMS *Ark Royal* in Gibraltar, and from all points of view – the Navy, Central Television, and Howerd himself – it was a great success. At the age of seventy-four Frankie Howerd could still delight an audience of servicemen and women.

4 Benny Hill: The long struggle to the top

When he was demobbed in 1947 Benny Hill had only one end in view: to become a professional entertainer, but first he had to find someone who would employ him.

One passport to success was to appear at the Windmill in London's West End. This little theatre in Windmill Street, Soho, owned and run by Vivian Van Damm, had the proud slogan "We never closed", having kept going throughout the war. Its great attraction was that it featured unclothed maidens who, the law decreed, were not allowed to move. They were in effect living statues in tableaux of various artistic scenes: Diana the huntress, Lady Godiva, the rape of the Sabines, anything that could include naked nymphs was presented and while the scenes were changed comedians kept the crowd, if not happy, then at least at bay. The shows ran continuously for twelve hours daily using several teams of girls, and for the comedians it was a baptism of fire. The randy audience fighting for the seats near the stage was not interested in the drolls who were there to entertain them.

The going was tough, so Van Damm needed a constant supply of inexpensive comics and held regular auditions. Having experienced it myself I know the terror of walking onto that small Windmill Street stage to stutter out the first joke and be told from the darkness of the stalls, where the sole arbiter Van Damm sat, Solomon like, "Thank you. Next please." This meant, of course, that you had failed.

That's what happened to Benny. After choking out his first gag he received the inexorable "Next please" and in seconds found himself in the street again. A lesson many ex-service entertainers learned was that while Army/RAF/Navy jokes brought the house down with service audiences, civilian entertainers were expected to offer a little more.

Those who had survived a Windmill audition and who appeared in the slogging six shows a day, six days a week routine include many who became stars: Jimmy Edwards, Dick Emery, Morecambe and Wise, Harry Worth and

Robert Moreton, whose diffident quotations from his Bumper Fun Book took him briefly to the top in the radio show *Educating Archie* and who subsequently committed suicide when his career faltered. But for all those who did pass the audition many more failed and vanished into the oblivion of respectability. Not that Van Damm was always right; many comedians he rejected were later to make the big time. Not only Benny Hill, but Bob Monkhouse and Norman Wisdom as well.

At the time of his unsuccessful Windmill audition Benny had always billed himself as Alf Hill, but fancied something a little more upmarket such as Leslie or Vernon. It was his brother Leonard who suggested Benny, Jack Benny being one of his idols, so Alf duly became Benny Hill. (Incidentally, as a footnote to the business of showbusiness names, Jack Benny, born Benjamin Kubelsky, first billed himself Ben K Benny and only later as Jack Benny.)

It is possible that one of the things which motivates the would-be professional funny man to change his name derives from the fact that he wishes to divorce himself from his *real* self and become a fictitious person in keeping with his fictitious material. In other words, distancing himself from reality, or perhaps blame if the material is badly received – as if to say it isn't *me*, Alfred Hill, it's *him*, Benny Hill.

Meanwhile, Benny Hill, living in cheap digs in London and desperate for work, found not what he sought, perhaps, but what was available in working men's clubs and pubs which featured live entertainment. The working men's clubs were about as glamorous as an Albanian pigeon loft and the pay was meagre, averaging £1 per performance. This was a time, remember, before television drove people out of the clubs and back home to watch the flickering screen and before the infinite boredom of watching the flickering screen night after night drove them back to the karaoke and drag acts of live entertainment in the pubs of the 1990s.

In the 1940s and early 1950s the working men's club was one of the few places a young comedian could earn a living, and while not all clubs gave the entertainers a good reception, enough did to keep hope alive, and a return booking meant success.

Benny Hill used these experiences to hone his material and develop an ability to swap repartee with the audience. To a noisy interrupter: "There's a bus leaving in two minutes – be under it." Another of his quips (indeed not original when he first used it) was to ask people returning from the lavatory, "Could you hear us in there? No? Well, we could hear you!" A joke he was still using in the very last TV show he ever made, when, as a vast Southern belle in a parody of *A Streetcar Named Desire*, he emerged from the powder room (the American euphemism for lavatory) to be asked the same question. It is probable that for the rest of his career (nearly forty-five years) he dusted off that same joke many many times. He certainly recycled his material endlessly and it is one of the puzzles of his worldwide success that his audiences never seemed to mind the endless repetitions of these retreads.

The five shilling comic worth 7s 6d in 1941 had become the £1-a-go comic trailing round London by bus and tube desperately trying to survive. There were moments he went upmarket. In 1947 he appeared at the Twentieth Century Theatre in Notting Hill Gate in a revue called *Spotlight* which featured another aspiring entertainer, Bob Monkhouse. They weren't paid, it being a "showcase" where agents could have a look at the potential talent. Benny, heartened by the audience reaction to his performance, tried the Windmill once more, but was again rebuffed with the usual "Next please" from the stony-hearted Van Damm.

It is hard to see why Van Damm accepted some comedians and rejected others, particularly as each of the successful aspirants remembers the indifference of the audience and sparseness of the laughs. Anyway Benny's second "no" at the Windmill didn't dishearten him and it was back to the grind of Dagenham, Harlesden, Lambeth, and Stoke Newington working men's clubs where in a good week he could make £5. Then things started to get better. His act was improving. The harsh environment of the clubs had helped him to polish the rough edges off his performance, and the sly asides, the knowing winks and the character cameos which were to make him a star later on were becoming more assured. In early 1948 he had graduated to Masonic dinners at three guineas a night.

By now ex-Colonel Stone had become a theatrical agent, and remembering how funny he had found Benny in Germany signed him up. From then on until he died Benny had the Richard Stone organisation behind him and as Richard Stone was among the cleverest and most respected of the agents, who could if pressed have sold sand to Saudi Arabia, Benny could not have found a better supporter and promoter. The first task was to get Benny out of the masonic dinners and into the professional theatre. Stone persuaded Hedley Claxton, an impresario who specialised in seaside shows – summer seasons – that Benny Hill would be a perfect feed for Hedley Claxton's star comedian, Reg Varney. Incidentally, Benny Hill did have one important hurdle to surmount before he clinched the job, an audition. But he beat the other close contender, an impressionist by the name of Peter

Gaytime – 1948. Reg Varney kneeling, Benny at the back grinning

Sellers, on the strength of an English calypso which he wrote and sang to his own guitar accompaniment.

Reg Varney was pleased with his new partner and the 1948 edition of *Gaytime* – no-one considered this an odd title in 1948 – at the Cliftonville Lido (a theatre of middling size in Kent) was a big success.

Before the main season *Gaytime* went on tour. As well as playing straight man to Reg Varney, Benny had his own solo spot, but once again that gap between the semi-professional and the truly professional was hard to bridge. This single spot was far from effective and, according to Reg Varney, Benny hated doing it. Being a comedian of any kind is a nervy business and one often finds the most brilliant performers in a state of shock. Reg Varney has always been the most sensitive of men and one can well imagine the tension in *Gaytime* as he and Hill tried to come to terms with their own, highly individual temperaments.

Fortunately their routines together worked extremely well and Varney was full of praise for his young feed who, like all good supporting players, appeared to do nothing while bringing a subtle authority to his work. Their *pièce de résistance* was a sketch in which Reg Varney, a small, perky, elfin performer, played a shy female tennis player with Benny Hill as the tennis instructor. In his book *The Benny Hill Story*, John Smith quotes Reg Varney saying that Hedley Claxton "took one look at it and declared it a disaster". But it went on and thanks to the skill of Varney and Hill it became the hit of the show, with Varney darting about the stage like a demented Monica Seles (though more petite) and Benny using a variety of facial expressions and much eye-rolling.

The team of Reg Varney and Benny Hill did three seasons of *Gaytime* before being signed by George and Alfred Black for the touring version of a London Palladium revue called *Sky High*, which had starred Jimmy Edwards. Edwards, another of that galaxy of ex-servicemen who had passed the Windmill's audition and emerged as post-war stars, was helped by the fact that his early scripts were written by Frank Muir. Edwards himself was not only an MA, but a war hero having won the DFC (Distinguished Flying Cross) whilst a Wing Commander in the RAF. He was also very self-confident, not to say arrogant, and it was only years later, when he "came out" and admitted he was gay that one realised his hearty, fox-hunting bluster was a facade.

Marty Feldman and I wrote for him in mid-career – his *and* ours – and I remember remarking to Marty how similar Edwards' reactions were to those of Frankie Howerd who was known to us as being homosexual.

But of all this more later. For the moment we're on tour with Reg Varney and Benny Hill in 1950 in a revue called *Sky High*.

Again Benny Hill's solo spot was the weak link in the show and if he had hated it in Cliftonville, where, to be honest, the good people on holiday would have laughed at almost anything, he must have loathed doing his stuff to the harder-to-please audiences of industrial England.

In fact, in Sunderland he got the bird. That's to say the audience didn't take to him, greeted him at first with silence, then jeers and then the ultimate put-down, the slow handclap. Benny Hill was desolated. He was so upset he resigned from the show and left the next week. Reg Varney was deeply upset to lose his feed and friend, but Benny was adamant. "What are you going to do?" asked Varney. "I don't know," said Hill, "... I'll think of something." This I suppose one could say, echoing the *Goon Show*, is where the Benny Hill story really starts.

It is difficult for the non-performer to understand the terrors that facing an audience can produce. The fear of failure is at the back of the mind and every joke is a mountain to be climbed. At the summit, if they laugh you are a success but with the next joke it is back to the bottom of the mountain and the same identical perilous climb to the peak and the next laugh. When they

Paris by Night – Kilburn by day

don't laugh the comedian plunges into an abyss and must desperately struggle to regain the audience's interest and approbation.

Looking back at the nearly forty-five years of success that Benny Hill enjoyed it is hard to realise that this terror lurked even in *him*, but fear, generated in his early career, and the occasions when he failed, must have gone in deep and given him the determination that once he was a success he would never slip back to the horrors of the slow handclap at Sunderland. That is perhaps why you find in Benny Hill's work the same jokes appearing again and again. They may be old, but, as a wise old comedian once said to me, "The only old joke is one that you have heard before." Come to that, people don't really mind hearing the same joke again if they find it funny.

My only argument with Benny Hill has been that in his later years many of the jokes were *not* funny. Benny Hill, however, who right to the end came across as a genial, amusing person with a twinkle in his eye and mischief in his soul, *was* funny. For that one could put up with any number of damp squibs.

In the early 1950s Benny Hill had not found his métier. Oh, he had jokes enough and a number of character cameos in his repertoire, but there was no central theme, nothing to remember him by. Frankie Howerd's early appearances were electrifying, and by finding a first-class writer in Eric Sykes he was able to extend and develop his range.

Benny Hill, on the other hand, was just another joke-teller. Thanks to Richard Stone he was now earning a decent living, but had yet to break through.

Here is a BBC report on Benny Hill, dated 10 October 1947:

> RONALD WALDMAN: The only trouble with him was that he didn't make me laugh *at all* – and for a comedian that's not very good. It's a mixture of lack of comedy personality and lack of comedy material.
>
> HARRY PEPPER: Joy Russell Smith gave him a good send him [sic] off as he has done a good show on *Band Box*. I find him without personality and very dully unfunny.
>
> VERNON HARRIS: Passable material, but he has a quite unfunny personality and so just doesn't come over.
>
> Grade 4
>
> As he has had a broadcast in *Band Box* and *Beginners, Please* is now passed for broadcasting.

So much for the BBC's reaction to Benny Hill on radio, but television would not be long in coming into its own. Restarting after the war, television could at first only attract tiny audiences as reception was possible only for a radius of twenty miles from the transmitter at Alexandra Palace, and sets were expensive and not that reliable. Unsurprisingly customers were reluctant to buy – reluctant that is until 1953 when the entire Coronation of Queen Elizabeth II was covered by television.

That single event transformed the listening and viewing habits of the British nation (and by the late 1950s, incidentally, caused the demise of the music halls). From now on TV was *the* thing and the *big* things on TV were panel games and variety shows. In the early 1950s Benny realised that TV gobbled up material and what could have lasted a music hall act a lifetime on the theatrical circuit was gone in a trice once shown on TV. With this in mind, in 1951 Benny Hill wrote a mass of material and submitted it in person to Ronnie Waldman – the same Ronnie Waldman who had said of Hill a few short years before: "... he didn't make me laugh *at all*..."

Waldman asked Benny Hill to act one of his sketches in his office and was so impressed he gave him a TV series. Such speed would be impossible today, but in the early 1950s TV's thirst for material was insatiable. So, Benny Hill was *in* and, barring a couple of hiccups, was to be *"in"* for the rest of his life.

5 *Howerd on tour and on TV*

*B*ack from his Far East tour Frankie Howerd made his TV debut on 11 January 1952. The show, *The Howerd Crowd*, with the Beverley Sisters, and a script by Eric Sykes, was well received by critics and public. Frankie said, in his autobiography, "All I remember of it was that it contained a sketch poking fun at the trendy TV cooks of the day."

Too many cooks? Frankie and friend in an early TV appearance

After the next Howerd show, on 8 March 1952, Cecil McGivern, the Controller of TV Programmes, wrote to his Head of Light Entertainment (or H.O.L.E. as it was known in BBC vernacular), Ronnie Waldman:

> Frankie Howerd is a television natural ... but ... This second programme was disappointingly below the standard of the first.

Howerd himself was far from happy, saying, "In truth my performance was not as good as it might have been ... So perhaps I wasn't right for TV in those days or maybe TV wasn't right for me."

Howerd complained that the programme was televised (live) in such a way that he couldn't see the audience and because of cameras, microphone booms etc., the audience couldn't see him. Hence there wasn't much laughter. It was "absolute murder", Howerd recalled in his autobiography. "The Americans solved the problem very simply. They didn't bother with studio audiences and just dubbed in the laughter." This might have been true of some American comedies (it was certainly the case with the 1960s/1970s success Rowan and Martin's *Laugh In*), but in the early days of US television they did use studio audiences. The studios were often converted theatres, the audience sat in the circle, the technology was in the stalls and thus out of the eye line of the audience. Another technique was to put the cameras on zoom lenses *behind* the audience.

But in 1952 the BBC Light Entertainment people were still feeling their way and often the artists suffered. However, not all was gloom. In December Howerd appeared, with great success, in the TV *Christmas Day Party*, and on 29 December Ronnie Waldman wrote to him at the London Palladium:

> Dear Frank,
>
> This letter is to say two things –
>
> First, my very sincere and grateful thanks for the superb job you did at our Christmas Party. I was very sorry indeed that you had to leave so quickly afterwards because I wanted to express my thanks and congratulations in person. You gave us a tremendous and really outstanding performance and it seems to be the general consensus of opinion that you "topped" the show in every way.
>
> This, of course, leads me to my second point. The "fuss and bother" we had about this show was most unfortunate. I do want you to realise that we are more than alive to your tremendous potential value on Television, but we want *you* to realise that we are not all complete clots

(even though we may sometimes look it!) and that when we build a show like the Christmas Party, we build it with the greatest possible care both for the sake of the show and for the sake of the artists.

Even though you weren't prepared to see it, the spot we gave you in that show was the perfect spot for you and, what is more, nobody but you could have held it. I personally have been in show business long enough (all my working life, in fact) not to make mistakes about elementary things like running-orders, and I would feel a whole lot happier if I could see signs of the fact that you were prepared to trust us a bit more to know our own job. If I make a mess of you, I deserve to be sacked, but I haven't yet – and Christmas Day was, to say the least, the very opposite!

I sincerely hope that 1953 will be a happier year for both of us. No more "fusses", no more arguments, a little more belief from you that we *do* know what is right and what is wrong for Television, a little more understanding from us about your own particular nervous approach to your work and your desire for perfection (which we share) and a whole heap of TV successes starring Frankie Howerd.

> Yours
> Ronald Waldman

In February 1953 producer T. Leslie Jackson wrote:

Dear Frankie,

Been meaning to write to you all the week and never got around to it, just to say how very grateful we were for the really terrific performance you put up on *What's My Line?*

We have never had a better "Celebrity" (and that includes Bob Hope). Wish we had seen you afterwards but understand you had to dash away.

Good luck and, on behalf of seven million viewers, many thanks.

> Yours sincerely
> T. Leslie Jackson

In his autobiography, Frankie Howerd omitted to mention his success as a guest on *What's My Line* in February 1953, but made much of his total failure as a panelist replacing Gilbert Harding in March 1954. He ascribed this to being unable to contribute spontaneous ad lib chat: "I went to pieces with nerves."

SOUVENIR OF THE
FABULOUS NEW
Folies Bergère
REVUE
"Pardon My
French"
AT THE PRINCE OF WALES THEATRE

COBB

FRANKIE HOWERD

FRANKIE HOWERD
SUNNY ROGERS
LEE YOUNG

Frankie's first big West End success

Later in 1953, came his first radio series written by Galton and Simpson, and a TV show called *Nuts In May*, which the *Daily Express* called "a triumph". The same year saw his first film, *The Runaway Bus*, in which he co-starred with Margaret Rutherford. They became great friends – even making a recording of "Nymphs and Shepherds" together. *The Runaway Bus* was a box office success and Howerd was on top of the world. In September he opened at London's Prince of Wales Theatre in the Bernard Delfont revue, *Pardon My French*, with Sunny Rogers, and his friend and "feed" Lee Young.

During the run of *Pardon My French*, Frankie was introduced to Johnny Speight, a dance band drummer and part-time insurance salesman who wanted to become a scriptwriter. I'll leave the story of their first meeting for Johnny to write in his autobiography, but it is enough here to say that he sold his first joke to Howerd. It went: "I'm livid. They're pulling down my house to build a slum."

I first met Frankie Howerd in 1955 on a variety bill at the Congress Theatre, Eastbourne. He asked me politely if I'd like some help with my make-up. I replied, equally politely, that I didn't. We became friendly, each telling the other of our families – in his case his mother and sister, Betty, in mine my wife and children. We all came to know each other much better in the years to come and, though there was a falling out some time later when a careless remark I had made was repeated to him and he felt affronted, we remained on good terms until the end.

At that Eastbourne date he asked me to stooge for him, that is to say to stand at the back of the auditorium during his act and shout a remark at a given moment. By doing that twice-nightly, and again the following week in Taunton, I came to know his act very well and admire his technique and timing, which were brilliant.

Later in London we visited each other's homes, walked the streets of Kensington together when he was anxious about his career, and many years later when I was in hospital recovering from an operation for cancer, and feeling pretty miserable, he visited me more than once, was kindness itself to my wife, and offered me the use of a house he then owned in Malta for my convalescence.

By that time I knew Frankie Howerd very well, had written for him solo, and with Marty Feldman, had sympathised with him when he was down, and rejoiced for him when his fortunes rose again.

"I'm from Brazil – where the nuts come from"

There is no doubt that in his forty-six years in the business he was more up than down and got through a remarkable quantity and variety of work. He was extremely adventurous and although he had more than his fair share of flops he also clocked up an impressive list of successes.

He was careless about his appearance, unlike Benny Hill who off stage was always beautifully dressed, well-tailored and immaculate. Howerd, too, could look good and his suits were expensive, but somehow he always seemed as if he had slept in them and carried this unkempt look onto the stage.

This apparent disorderliness in appearance and material was actually well thought out. He did not wish to be "theatrical" but "ordinary" like the people he entertained, and his tastes in other things were remarkably simple. He preferred steak and kidney pudding or oxtail stew to more exotic dishes, and when I first met him he was a virtual teetotaller, his tipple being a weak mixture of sherry and tonic water. He enjoyed a night at the dogs and would frequently invite friends to the old White City stadium, now the site of a BBC office block and known by its inmates as "the biscuit box".

The greyhound racing bit was more pleasant than it sounds as one sat in a smart restaurant overlooking the track and uniformed lackeys placed one's bets and returned with the winnings – on the rare occasions one did win – while the white wine and smoked salmon were consumed and Frankie chattered to one and all.

Although, as I have said, he was adventurous in his choice of roles, when trouble struck he tended to return to his roots and to old and favoured material. In his very last recorded show, he was still telling the joke about the woman brought into the hospital because her legs wouldn't move. She's wheeled in to see the doctor and two minutes later walks out unaided. He asks the doctor, "What was the matter with her?" "Nothing," says the doctor, "the silly cow had both legs down the one knicker." When I heard Howerd tell that joke in 1947 I reckoned it to be past its sell-by date, but the 1991 audience of doctors and nurses in a Nottingham hospital whooped and roared their approval and gave it a round of applause. Not perhaps in the best possible taste but in Howerd's hands – funny.

On the subject of taste, Howerd said, in an interview with Gloria Hunniford on BBC radio:

> To be vulgar is not the same as being filthy, tasteless and offensive. But taste is a matter of opinion. Comedy is like walking through a minefield.

And to BBC producer, John Browell, in another radio interview:

I don't believe in analysing what you do ... It's a mistake to analyse. You lose your naturalness. It's very difficult to assess oneself. Am I bawdy? Some people might think so and some people might be right.

But then what is the secret of making people laugh? Frankie Howerd answered one questioner:

There is a route and you stumble on it. You want to entertain, to please people and you find a way of doing it.

and in BBC TV's *Arena* in 1990 he said to June Whitfield:

After all, one man's meat is another man's poison – you can't please everybody.

Indeed, in 1955, after one broadcast, the Director-General of the BBC received the following:

There was a performance by a man named Frankie Howerd broadcast on television from the Radio Show. As far as I could gather he was giving the viewing audience as well as those who were present a lesson on how to make love.

He was practising his idea of the art upon an adult-size rag doll. In my view and in the view of the others who happened to be looking at the same time in my house, some of the gestures bordered on the obscene.

The unanimous opinion of myself and my friends was that we did not wish that kind of thing brought into our own homes. It was quite indefensible.

The BBC did defend it, of course, probably along the lines of "It's all in the eye of the beholder", and "No offence was intended."

Before long Howerd was to put behind him (for the time being) the limited pleasures of stand-up comedy and go legit. That's to say, he appeared on television in the old Aldwych farce, *Tons of Money*, with Eleanor Summerfield and Jack Melford.

This was a success and he followed it with a version of *Charley's Aunt* for H. M. Tennent, which opened at the Globe Theatre in Shaftesbury Avenue in December 1955, and after a three-month run to full houses went on tour. Both the London run and the tour were enlightened by the presence of the actor (long since turned comedy scriptwriter and guru) Richard Waring.

Now, Waring is a great giggler (as I recorded in my book *A Point Of View*, remembering the time we had an hysterical year together at the Strand Theatre in the revue *For Adults Only*) and would break into helpless giggles, on stage, at the drop of a hat. He found Howerd hilarious and Howerd was lured into that strange world of helpless laughter which lies halfway between hysteria and lunacy, known as "corpsing", which can affect actors for no particular reason. The late Lord Olivier was also said to be a great giggler and it can be very infectious or deeply irritating, depending on one's mood. However, there it was, Howerd and Waring shrieking with laughter throughout a triumphant run of *Charley's Aunt*.

Then came the offer of another Bernard Delfont West End spectacular, *Plaisirs de Paris*, which Howerd turned down, a decision which, he said later, was "the worst error of judgment I was to make in my entire life."

But for the moment the future looked rosy for Howerd the actor, as he was asked to appear as Bottom in *A Midsummer Night's Dream* at the Old Vic.

6 *Down but not out*

*I*f Frankie Howerd was "twitchy" when it came to playing with such distinguished actors as Coral Browne, Edward Hardwicke and Paul Daneman, his Bottom in that production of *A Midsummer Night's Dream* was a success. "Most poetic," said *The Times*.

But there followed a series of misjudgments on Howerd's part that caused his audience to desert him. His success as Bottom led him to take more up-market roles, such as in a TV version of Molière's *School For Wives*. Not many oohs and aahs in that, and the audience weren't happy to see their erstwhile hero as a seventeenth-century, scheming, bald-headed lecher.

Actually, by this time in his career Frankie Howerd's hair had receded so much that he resorted to a toupée. Perhaps Stanley Dale had got it for him cheap but, costly or not, it came to be known by those of us who wrote for him at the time as the "dead ferret". It did look as if some poor mangy animal had crawled onto his head and died there.

For outdoor wear he sported a pork pie hat, and the story is told of his emerging from the stage door to greet his fans at the variety theatre at New Brighton, when, through no fault of his own in a very high wind, both hat and toupée flew off his head, and he disappeared rapidly to the seclusion of his dressing room until the embarrassment wore off.

I never saw him without his toupée and still wonder if a false hairpiece, like a name change, gave him, as it were, an alter ego, a toupéed Frankie Howerd who could perform acts that the balding Francis Howard could not.

Curiously enough the last time I saw Frankie Howerd in costume was in 1990 at an historical pageant organised by Gyles Brandreth. We were all dressed as Kings of England (I was one of the early ones, Eggfroth or somesuch) and Frankie in costume and make-up made a very impressive Richard III. When one considers how successful many of his period characterisations were in later years it is surprising that the early TV audiences didn't rise to the fact that their hero was showing another facet of his versatility.

"My Bottom was the talk of London"

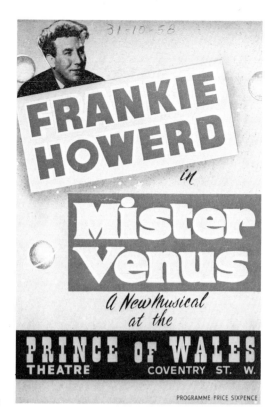

The seventeen-day wonder

But in 1958 they didn't, and worse came in the shape of a dire musical called *Mr Venus* written by Alan Melville, the doyen of revue writers. But far from the gay ironies of Melville's work for Hermione Gingold (*Sweet and Low*, *Sweeter and Lower* and *Sweetest and Lowest*), *Mr Venus* seems by all accounts to have been a quasi-religious tract in which Anton Diffring, in a sequinned jockstrap and wings, arrived on earth to save mankind.

How Howerd got mixed up in it Heaven knows, but he did. Alan Melville took his name off the credits and in spite of last-minute rewrites by Ray Galton, Alan Simpson, and Johnny Speight, *Mr Venus* was a disaster on tour and didn't survive in the West End beyond seventeen performances.

Kenneth Adam, Controller of Programmes at the BBC, wrote to his Head of Light Entertainment:

> The disappearance of *Mr Venus* presumably leaves Frankie Howerd without
> work. I have considerable interest in this comedian. Do not let us be
> slow in seeing if we can make use of him.

But the BBC Drama department stepped in before the Light Entertainment department, and the immensely experienced Rudolph Cartier asked Howerd to repeat his role in *A Midsummer Night's Dream* on television. Unfortunately the recording date clashed with his already-contracted summer season and the offer had to be declined. Earlier the Outside Broadcast unit had wanted to film the rustic scene from the Old Vic production, but there again facilities and dates proved impossible to reconcile and no recording was made. (Some time later *A Midsummer Night's Dream* was made by Thames Television, and Bottom was played by Benny Hill).

Yet another flop was on its way, a film this time, a sequel to a British comedy about a down-at-heel Royal Navy ship, called *Up the Creek*. It made some money largely because Peter Sellers starred in it as an unscrupulous naval petty officer, and in 1959 a follow-up was quickly ordered and reached the cinemas in 1960. It was titled, with the subtlety for which British comedies are noted, *Further Up the Creek*, with Howerd replacing Sellers. It did very bad business.

A short while later he accepted the leading part in a TV one-off, written by the Canadian, Reuben Ship, and called *Shakespeare Without Tears*. Although well received, you must take my word that it was a mediocre script, but Frankie fitted the part and it worked. It was a broad farce and told the story of a stagestruck shop assistant who dreams of playing Shakespeare, is sacked, gets a job as a dresser at the Old Vic, impersonates the star, is discovered, but saves the day by accepting the role of seducer of a female fan of the star and confessing to a "liaison" to the woman's outraged husband. Even writing it down you can feel the plot creak but, believe me, it was very much worse than I have described.

With the success of Reuben Ship's *Shakespeare Without Tears*, the Light Entertainment Group thought it would be a good idea for Ship and his uncredited co-writer, Phil Sharp, to write a series for Howerd, who was summoned by the deputy head of Light Entertainment at the BBC, Tom Sloan, and told that as he had a reputation for altering scripts, he was to be given the series only on the condition that he didn't alter a word.

This February 1959 letter from Eric Maschwitz (another H.O.L.E.) to Stanley Dale explains the situation fully.

> My dear Stanley,
>
> Following our conversation of yesterday morning I have now arranged for Phil Sharp and Reuben Ship to be at this office at 10.30 a.m. on Friday next for a discussion with Frankie Howerd.
>
> The situation, as I outlined it to you, is as follows. After carefully watching Frankie's last show I came to the conclusion that given more time and the opportunity of knowing our comedian better and discussing

the scripts with him both before and during the process of writing the writers could turn out a situation comedy series capable of showing Frankie at his very best (and that is very good).

I have spoken to the writers who would be interested to "have a go" as long as they could work with Frankie from the very start. This is, of course, the American method of operation which has led to such outstanding series as "I Love Lucy" and "Sergeant Bilko", on both of which Phil Sharp has been engaged. They are anxious, before undertaking any actual writing, to work out a firm "characterisation" for our hero (when they wrote the last script he was comparatively a stranger to them).

It was obvious from my talk with them that both writers would insist upon a sort of partnership with Frankie in the preparation of the scripts; they are used to and would therefore not resent receiving suggestions and intelligent criticism from the stars they work with; the sort of relationship which Hancock and Edwards both have with their writers. If I may be quite frank with you, Frankie has a reputation of being a little off-hand with writers and changing their scripts willy-nilly; if he were to insist upon doing this, then I think Ship and Sharp would not be interested in going ahead. Personally I hope and believe that Frankie will see the point of this. He is basically a very fine comedy actor – not just a stand-up "mugger" like so many of them – and should be prepared to regard the situation comedy scripts as plays rather than routines, with a basis of truth and character and himself as the one man larger than life in a real world.

I look forward to our meeting on Friday. I hope that it will be successful as it is my wish, if it can be managed, that Frankie should follow Tony Hancock in a series of six or seven half-hour programmes in early April when we can make the series one of our Big Guns for the Spring.

Yours as ever,

Eric Maschwitz
Head of Light Entertainment, Television

Now, that may well have been acceptable if the writers had been Galton and Simpson (and I suspect that in the years they wrote for Tony Hancock he rarely altered a thing), but the two men contracted to write for Howerd didn't really know him.

Here again one comes up against either the deliberate suppression of facts or an extraordinary lapse of memory. I could find no-one among Frankie Howerd's managers or friends who remembered the series or its name.

Once again the BBC Written Archives at Caversham solved the problem and after some detective work came up with the title *Frankly Howerd*, the dates May–June 1959, and the odd fact that only Reuben Ship was credited. There is a note in a BBC file quoting what the writers are to be paid but no other trace remains of either Sharp or Ship.

In his autobiography Howerd dismisses the incident as follows:

> Tom Sloan said, "You've got a very bad reputation for altering scripts. You must give me your word of honour that you won't change anything." "What's all this about reputation?" I countered. "All I've ever done is discuss with scriptwriters ways of making a script more Howerdish... I don't know where this *reputation* comes from."

With the advantage of hindsight, and my good friends at Caversham, I can offer three examples of BBC thinking. The first is from February 1948.

From: Acting Controller, Light Programme

Subject: VARIETY BANDBOX:
SUNDAY, 22nd FEBRUARY 1948

To: Head of General Overseas Programmes 23
February, 1948

Did you hear Variety Bandbox on Sunday?

Frankie Howerd was obviously screamingly funny to the local audience with a lot of business that did not mean a thing to the listeners. It meant so much to him, however, that his stooge dried up at one point, and he himself got completely lost in his script soon after.

If you agree with me, you will no doubt want to take this up with H.V.

T. W. Chalmers

OPPOSITE Norman Wisdom, Bill Fraser, Frankie and Marjorie Holmes
in the 1951 radio show *Fine Goings On*

The second dates from 1951.

From: Assistant to H.V.

Subject: FINE GOINGS ON   12 January 1951

To: Mr Tom Ronald HV

Copy to: A.H.V. (P)
           Variety Booking Manager
           Mr Bryan Sears
           Miss Absalom

I am simply placing on record that the Frankie Howerd
Show is "all yours" as from the recording on
Sunday, 28th January.

                         C. J. Mahoney

[Handwritten:] And I would like to place on record
that Frankie Howerd is the most difficult artist I've
ever had to cope with.

                         Tom Ronald

The third is dated 19 April 1957.

From: Mr John Simmonds, 317 Aeolian Hall

Subject: THE FRANKIE HOWERD SHOW

To: A.H.V. (P) 19th April 1957

<u>URGENT   CONFIDENTIAL</u>

Before I went on leave, I wrote to Frankie Howerd (copy attached) as you suggested. I received no reply, so after approximately ten days, my secretary phoned Mrs. Vertue to enquire what had happened.

   It appears that the letter was pocketed by Stanley Dale and, according to Mrs. Vertue, had not reached Frankie Howerd himself. She would, however, see that it did. Subsequently, I received a garbled message via Eric Merriman* (goodness knows why!) to say that I would be contacted later.

   By now, however, I was about to go on leave (on August 2nd) so I made arrangements for Frankie Howerd to contact you in my absence, as clearly time was getting short. I gather that he has failed to do so and in my opinion the situation has become farcical, if not insulting, both to you, myself and the Corporation. He must either be a very bad businessman, mentally unstable or just not interested. I wouldn't like to commit myself as to which is the case and I feel that the hopes of a successful series are very slender if this is the way we are to begin. May I suggest that we cancel it before it gets any worse?

John Simmonds

* Eric Merriman was a client of Associated London Scripts at that time, writing with Lew Schwarz

What the outcome was I have no idea as most of the protagonists are dead or have forgotten the various incidents. However the fact remains that, like it or not, Frankie Howerd had got himself a reputation for being difficult.

Now comes the memory lapse regarding *Frankly Howerd*:

> "What did I get?" asked Howerd rhetorically.
>
> "Two writers; an American and a Canadian. One had never written for me before, the other had never even heard of me, far less seen me perform. Result, excellent scripts but just not me."

In the TV light entertainment that failed – *Frankly Howerd*

As a matter of fact the series was dire both in writing and performance. The following memos and letters show very fully the BBC's position:

From: Head of Light Entertainment Television
Eric Maschwitz

Subject: SITUATION COMEDY SERIES   25th May 1959

To: Controller of Programmes Tel.

Copy: Assistant Head of Light Entertainment Tel.
(Tom Sloan)

The poor quality of the present Frankie Howerd series is causing me a great deal of concern. Like yourself when you asked me to see what could be done with Howerd I had hoped that he might be able to make a come-back, particularly in view of the promise shown by his "Old Vic" comedy broadcast on 28th January.

I engaged the same experienced writers for his series
but unfortunately they came up against the problem
of a neurotic performer unable to make up his mind
whether he wants to be a slapstick comedian or a
comic actor. If they may have failed in their job,
there can be no doubt that the producer, Harry
Carlisle, has worked hard and loyally to make the
best of a disturbing situation. Things might have
gone better had Messrs Norden and Muir already been
available for script supervision or had the L.E.
Script Section, for which I have asked, been in
existence.

In presenting the situation to you I am *not*
attempting to disclaim responsibility. I do feel,
however, that the time has come for us to face up to
the woeful shortage of performers and, even more
desperate, of writers in the most difficult field of
"situation comedy".

From: Head of Light Entertainment Television

Subject: L.E. OFFERS   25 July 1960

To: H.P.P. Tel

Copy: C.P. Tel., A.H.L.E. Tel., CA(G)L.E.

In reply to your memo of July 20th:-
1. With regard to C.P. Tel.'s doubts as to the
acceptability of FRANKIE HOWERD for "Music Hall"
in Week 39, I personally feel that this artist can
give us good value now that he has returned to his
old "Variety Bandbox" formula of stand-up spots with
a single sketch; I will admit that he did not
succeed in situation comedy and am happy to say that
he has now apparently given up his ambition to be an
actor.

18 January 1961

Dear Frankie,

   I am sorry to have to tell you that Mr Kenneth Adam, our
Controller of Programmes, has decided to terminate the run of
"LAUGHLINE" as of last night. He is not satisfied that this programme
has measured up to the high standard recently set by BBC Light

Entertainment, but of course this decision is in no way a reflection on your personal contribution to the Series.

Our Bookings Department will be settling all fees immediately.

Yours sincerely,

Tom Sloan
Assistant Head of Light Entertainment
Television

By the end of 1961 Tom Sloan had lost his greatest asset, Tony Hancock, to commercial television (a move which led, inevitably, to Hancock's decline and fall and eventual suicide, alone, in Sydney, Australia) and he asked Ray Galton and Alan Simpson what or for whom they now wished to write. "Frankie Howerd," they said, to which Tom Sloan replied, "Forget him, he's finished. Write ten playlets and we'll pick one and make it into a series." They wrote the series and called it *The Galton and Simpson Playhouse* which had a different cast in a different story each week. The one that became a series was the story of two rag-and-bone men constantly bickering but held together by their mutual need for each other. It was, of course, *Steptoe and Son*.

Beryl Vertue had been looking after Howerd for some time, the mysterious Stanley Dale having totally vanished (she was even looking after Jim Dale and got him his first *Carry On* film role), but people were not anxious to book Frankie Howerd for anything and by 1961 he was at a low ebb.

It must have been two years earlier when I got to know him well, although, as I have said, I worked with him on variety bills in the mid-1950s and we had become moderately friendly. He was deeply troubled and after I had finished my day's stint writing (with Eric Merriman) *Beyond Our Ken* for radio, and various variety programmes for TV, Frankie, with his boxer dog, Red, would turn up at the office we used at 12 Holland Villas Road and suggest that he and I should go for a walk, and walk we did. All round South Kensington as Frank poured out his woes, confessed to his penury and generally used me as a sounding board.

He had been booked in a summer season at Scarborough and I contributed some material at his request, a send-up of a Marilyn Monroe-type *femme fatale*, Frankie in drag being *fatale* maybe, but certainly no *femme*.

That season was an unhappy one for Frankie and woe seemed to pile on woe. A TV version of *Twenty Questions*, with Isobel Barnett, Muriel Young, Stephen Potter, and Stuart McPherson in the chair was a failure as was a stage version of *Alice in Wonderland* at the old Winter Garden theatre in London's

Drury Lane. But if 1959 had been bleak 1960 looked like being utterly barren and to top it all Frankie received an income tax demand for thousands of pounds of unpaid tax. Whoever was managing his affairs at the time, Stanley Dale I assume, was not doing it too well.

There was however one gleam of light amidst the encircling gloom. Dennis Heymer came into Frankie Howerd's life. Dennis became his personal manager, chauffeur and confidante. It was a friendship which was to last until the end. Dennis, dependable, understanding, infinitely loyal, was to make a great deal of difference to Frankie Howerd's life.

Previously Frankie's only true friends and confidants had been his mother and his sister, Betty, and his friend Lee Young. When his mother died and Lee Young had gone to Australia there was only Betty to turn to until Dennis appeared on the scene. They both gave their all to help Frankie through his traumatic years.

Let me describe Betty as I remember her, sitting in my home or acting as hostess when Frankie entertained. She was cheerful and gossipy, a good companion and a very welcome guest.

She was of medium height, with brown hair, much better looking than her brother, but with some of his wit and a wry sense of humour. My first wife, Dot, entertained them occasionally, my present wife (we're now nearing our thirtieth anniversary) entertained them frequently. On one occasion we had just returned from a motoring holiday in France, it was about six-thirty on a Sunday evening and we had travelled by a delayed hovercraft from Boulogne to Dover and thence to Hanover Gate, Regent's Park where we then lived.

We had just dumped our luggage in the hall when the phone rang. It was Frank. "Oh, Barry," he said, "we were wondering, only you see it's Dennis's night off and Betty and I, well, I wondered if it's not too much trouble ... if Betty and I could come round to supper."

I said we would love to see them, but that we were only just back from holiday and apart from a French loaf and a Camembert cheese there was no food in the house. There was a pause and a muffled exchange between brother and sister, then Frank said, "Oh, we'll bring the food. There's a little corner shop round here that's still open. We'll be right over."

And right over they came bearing a strange assortment of things to eat: a sliced loaf, tins of sardines, corned beef, baked beans, pea soup and a tinned sultana pudding.

My wife Lyn, and Betty made a very good meal out of this strange mixture and with it we drank our duty-free wine followed by duty-free brandy. It was

Frankie with two favourite ladies – Cilla Black and June Whitfield

the strangest alfresco meal I had ever eaten. When we were replete Frank said, "Oh, by the way, there's a programme I'd like to see on the telly. Only, our set's broken." So that was it! He specially wanted to watch a TV show and was even prepared to bring the meal that preceded it. It gets high marks for ingenuity.

Others tell similar stories. Cilla Black, on Frankie's *This Is Your Life*, remembered how he invited himself to Sunday lunch – roast lamb. It was at a time when they had appeared together in yet another of those Bernard Delfont spectacular revues and had been together on several TV "specials", and were good friends.

Every Sunday, it seems, Frankie Howerd would invite himself to lunch, until one weekend he said, "I won't be coming this Sunday." "Oh, why not?" asked Cilla. "Because I'm sick of roast lamb week after week. Why can't you have liver and bacon?"

In 1960 I started writing with Marty Feldman. We had met when we were both bottom-of-the-bill comedians, and some years of friendship had come and gone when we found to our surprise and delight that we could write scripts together. Not only write scripts, but write successful and even award-winning scripts.

Our chief employers at the time were Granada Television and our major contribution to the gaiety of nations was a TV series starring Alfie Bass and Bill Fraser, called *Bootsie and Snudge*. Our contract bound us exclusively to Granada only for TV work, but we were allowed to write for radio. Knowing this Frankie Howerd soon asked us for a script. We wrote one, a long monologue which he read without showing any emotion and then said, "Yes, it's very good, but where are the oohs and aahs?"

We said, "What?"

He said, "You know my style – ooh aah, what a funny woman, chilly, and all that."

We said, "We thought you ad libbed that."

"Oh, no," he said, "the writers put it in."

So we took the script back and wrote in "ooh, aah," "what a funny woman," "I'll just get myself comfy," and any other asides and ad libs we could think of. We sent him the result and he phoned to say, "Thanks, it's just right."

We were pleased with ourselves, as any young writers would be (this was 1961), but payment was a long time coming. Eventually I put it to Frankie: "Er ... what about the money for the script." He looked at me in astonishment and said: "You don't need money. Look what Granada are paying you." I said, "Ah, yes, but we are professional writers and professional writers get paid." He said "I'll tell you what. Stanley Dale made me buy a set of *Encyclopaedia Britannica* as an investment. They're no good to me. You take the encyclopaedias and give Marty a tenner." Which is what happened – and I still have the encyclopaedias, bound in a particularly nasty sort of plastic, and even after thirty years they still smell awful. I keep them in the spare room.

Later, when we were writing regularly for Frankie and payment was long overdue we sent the following parody of a tailor's bill:

ACCOUNT

TOOK AND FELDMAN

Scripts To The Nobility And Gentry

To: Supplying Four Scripts: -

To: Blocking, Filling, Sealing up the cracks, and plastering: -

To: keeping their heads when all about were losing theirs: -

To: replacement of damaged material in Programme Two, and replacing with new parts: -

To: making Blue Material: -

To: renovating customer's old material: -

To: making good Dry Rot: -

To: Materials (Paper, Typewriter Ribbon, Blood, Sweat and Tears): -

To: despatching the whole promptly, including cost of Transport and Packaging (e.g. Paper clips, Staples, Stout Manilla Binding): -

    Gratuities included — 15% Service Charge: -

                                TOTAL: - 40 guineas

The prompt payment of this will be much appreciated, in order to bring our books up to date.

All the items in this document are entirely fictitious, except the amount.

P.S. We are not charging you for the material in this letter — Neither does it constitute a contract.

We were paid (£42) for our four scripts by return.

It must be said that what kept Frankie Howerd going when his career appeared to be in tatters was the faith of two radio producers, Bill Worsley and John Browell, and of two young scriptwriters (Feldman and me) who had been told by the BBC Radio Light Entertainment hierarchy, Pat Hillyard and Jim Davidson, in a curious echo of what had been said to Galton and Simpson by the TV moguls, "Forget Frankie Howerd. He's finished. Find yourself a new, young comic and hang on to his coattails as he goes to the top." It was advice that we thought then was insulting and, looking back, completely out of touch. For although Frankie Howerd did have a very lean time for two or three years, the things that made him funny – his use of language, his understanding of people, his sensitivity, and his sense of mischief – never left him and it only needed a touch of good management, a little self-confidence and a bit of luck and he'd be right back at the top.

Those three things came to him through Beryl Vertue, Peter Cook and Ned Sherrin.

7 *Benny on TV*

*T*o describe a comedian's work without quoting him line by line and describing the visual jokes in detail is difficult. Even then it is only possible to give a general picture. The nuances of performance and personality are missing, even the vocal level; the half-muttered asides, the sudden fortissimo shouts can only be guessed at.

This is particularly true of Benny Hill, whose scripts when written down seem reasonably amusing, but not world beaters. Let me give you some examples.

> "How did you come to hurt your leg?"
> "I didn't come to hurt my leg, I came to mend the roof."

and

> "I gave my secretary the sack. She said, 'I'll do anything if you'll forgive me.' So, I forgave her four times."

Those two were quoted by Michael Billington in an article on Hill in *The Guardian*.

Mark Steyn, in the London *Evening Standard*, quoted a better example of Benny Hill's sense of humour, when, on *The Des O'Connor Show*, denying that he was a recluse and reading from his diary he said, "Went to showbiz party. Met Jim Davidson, a fine comedian and a gentleman. Talked to all three of them."

In a postcard from the Isle of Wight to Philip Jones, his long-time boss at Thames Television, he wrote, "The fun down here goes on some nights till half past eight... I arrived here just after the Bob Monkhouse show closed. Now where am I going to get some jokes for the next series?!!"

On another occasion he wrote to Philip Jones, from Madrid: "Last week in Nice I couldn't venture out without being stared at, photographed, asked for my autograph, and generally pestered. It really was quite worrying. I've been in Madrid for two days now and not a soul has noticed I'm here. It really is quite worrying."

71

For my money these are great improvements on many of the jokes he used in his radio and TV shows:

> We have a radio in every room in the house – except one. Well, you've got to have somewhere to go when Bob Monkhouse is on.

There was no real antagonism between Hill and Monkhouse, it was like the pseudofeud between American comedians – Jack Benny and Fred Allen.
Another of Hill's golden oldies was:

> My mother-in-law wears slacks. When she walks down the street it looks like two small boys fighting under a blanket.

(A joke I first heard told by Billy Russell in 1942.) And another:

> "His wife doesn't understand him."
> "Why not?'
> "She's Norwegian. They've been married ten years and only spoken six times. This year they're taking the six children on a picnic...'

And of an avant-garde film maker:

> "He now thinks he's a cat."
> "Oh? How does he clean himself?"
> "With great difficulty."

And then there's a joke which turns up with monotonous regularity, in various forms, in Hill's work. For instance:

> FEED: Look at that tree
> HILL: I can see it
> FEED: Look at the grass
> HILL: I can see it
> FEED: And look, look...
> HILL: (Exasperated) I can see it!
> FEED: Then why did you tread in it?

Then there are the orphan rice crispies – snap, crackle, but no pop.
The following jokes come from a TV programme made in December 1987. From the age of the jokes it could as easily have been 1887.

> "I hear your warehouse burnt down last night."
> "Shh! That's tomorrow."

"Can you explain the difference between unlawful and illegal?"
"Sure. Unlawful is against the law."
"And illegal?'
"Illegal is a sick bird."

"His father was in a fire last month."
"Was he badly burned?"
"They don't kid about at the crematorium."

In his early days on BBC TV Benny was a moderately good compère, delivered fairly amusing monologues, but really came into his own with impersonation. In the 1950s there were a great many "how to" programmes and among the presenters of these programmes were Barry Bucknell – king of DIY; Philip Harben – a bearded, fussy cookery expert; and the hairdresser Raymonde, known as Mr Teasy Weasy. It was on these personalities that Benny Hill based his skits, topping them all when he appeared (through trick photography) as all the members of the panel of *Juke Box Jury*, *What's My Line?*, and *Find The Link* (of this last more in a moment).

In those days when television was sparse, only one channel of BBC TV, no commercial television, and satellite and cable undreamt of, it was easy to become a personality. The viewers all watched the same programmes and the following morning discussed the merits or otherwise of what they had all seen the night before. So, Barbara Kelly's outsize earrings, Gilbert Harding's temperamental outbursts, Cliff Michelmore's benign handling of the links in the *Tonight* programme, Fanny Craddock, another cookery expert, looking more butch than butcher, with her husband Johnny lurking in the background, in tuxedo and with glass in hand, were all ripe for parody. Benny Hill parodied them all. In later years he went one step further. In 1968, Clifford Davis of the *Daily Mirror* told his readers: "In tonight's show he's going to do 'doubles', Elizabeth Taylor and Richard Burton, Mae West and W. C. Fields, plus Esther and Abi Ofarim."

In the 1950s Benny started to invent his own gallery of characters too, the best-known being Fred Scuttle (a bespectacled, moonfaced simpleton with delusions of adequacy!). All in all Benny had found a style that the public wanted, a comedian and impersonator who could mock his betters in a gentle way and could reduce the "gods" of the small screen to normal size.

Here, from that same 1987 show, from which I quoted a page or two back, is a moment from a restaurant sketch. Benny is the head waiter. The menu, he said, was inspired by the Famous and the Infamous (I wrote a similar

The universally-loved Fred Scuttle

routine for Val Doonican in 1980 based on the menu of the BBC Television Centre restaurant, the only dish I now remember is Pâté Boulaye!)

Anyway, here's the Benny Hill version of the dishes available:

EDWINA CURRY WITH ANNEKA RICE

MAGNUS PYKE

TORVILL AND DEAN

"What fish is that?" asks the diner. "Skate", answers Benny.

"I say," says the diner, "What is the SAMANTHA FOX?" Benny answers "A succulent, delicious game bird ... very tender, very tasty. Nice plump breast ... and it's served without dressing."

After the ogling the dialogue becomes uglier –

"What's the OLIVER REED?"

"A thick slice of ham."

"What is the ANNE DIAMOND?"

"Sheep's head with the brains taken out."

Which, for my money, is not only unfunny but gratuitously insulting.

Through his characterisations he could use material and say things that he as himself in a lounge suit couldn't. But where did all this material come from? The truth is that it came from a variety of sources. It is not possible to copyright an idea but by subtly twisting other people's inventions Benny Hill found a whole new area of material to be exploited.

Having no family *ties* (although deeply attached to his own family) and few responsibilities he was able to travel the world observing, noting, and, he said, turning what he had seen and noted into fresh comedy. Only it was not "fresh" comedy at all, but rehashed versions of other people's ideas. He also had a good memory and had grown to understand in his formative years that people, his audiences, actually preferred jokes they knew and routines they recognised.

Frankie Howerd once said to me: "If I told a completely new joke nobody would laugh. They wouldn't understand what was funny about it." Benny Hill obviously discovered this for himself and for the rest of his life kept studiously to material that was in some way familiar to his audiences. He was also cynical having learned what he described as the "insincere sincerity of showbusinesses".

Another trick he mastered early on was undercranking, that is shooting film at eighteen frames a second and printing the film at twenty-four frames a second. The action is speeded up and becomes jerky, just as we are used to seeing in the early silent movies. Part of the fun of these comedies was their faster-than-reality speed (just think of those Keystone Kops car chases). It was some time before the hand-cranked camera was replaced by electrically or motor-driven cameras and motion became more like normal life, but it is still possible to alter camera speeds to great comic effect, as Hill proved.

In his travels and in his many hours – in fact years – sitting in front of a television set he must have seen, remembered and reproduced almost every sight gag known to man.

He loved the circus and in his clown character paid homage to the circus ring. It is possible that his clown, with its echoes of the great Russian clown Arkady Raikin, Charlie Cairoli, and Coco, is the finest of Benny Hill's creations.

The item in which he strips right down to his skeleton and then piece by piece discards his skeletal head, torso and limbs with the final touch of a disembodied hand scuttling off screen is brilliant. I can think of no one who has bettered it.

He also had, it must be said, a dirty mind. That is his alter ego, the person he portrayed, had a dirty mind because I'm sure that the real Benny Hill, the one endlessly kind, thoughtful, a good conversationalist, generous and

sophisticated, the *off screen* Benny Hill, wasn't a bit like the creatures of his imagination. He escaped from reality through them, and audiences all over the world unconsciously understood this and through *The Benny Hill Show* were able to release some of their own secret pent-up feelings, wishes and desires.

This I think was Benny Hill's great achievement, but I wonder if he was aware of it.

Benny Hill is difficult to understand. He kept his TV appearances to a minimum, was "disgusted" by the vast amount of money he received for making TV commercials and spent the time, when he wasn't preparing for his next TV series, travelling. Thanks probably to Richard Stone's handling of his affairs, he never gave money a thought, and left at his death an estate valued at over seven million pounds (to be precise £7,548,192). It is doubtful if he knew what he was worth, or cared.

He was happiest alone or with one companion. He walked when he could have had a chauffeur-driven car at his disposal. He shopped simply in supermarkets and was quite indifferent to money. Just as long as he could work or travel as the mood took him he was content.

This unconcern for money started early in his career, as this 1949 letter from the BBC demonstrates:

> Benny Hill, Esq.,
> 62 Ambler Road,
> London.
>
> Dear Sir,
>
> On 9th July 1948 we sent you our cheque H 28665 for £5. 5. 0. in payment of the fee due to you for the reproduction on 1st July of "Listen my Children" originally recorded on 29th May (broadcast on 29th June).
>
> We have been notified by our Bank that you have not presented this cheque for payment and consequently it has now become out of date.
>
> Would you please return the cheque to us, or if you have no trace of it, inform us so we can arrange for a new cheque to be sent.
>
> Yours faithfully,
>
> for Programme Accountant

OPPOSITE In these moods I can crush a grape with my bare hands

I was in Madame Tussaud's one day in 1985 (doing some research before writing an article about the waxworks) and noted which of the wax effigies was most popular. There were many to choose from, including a tableau depicting the royal family at the wedding of the Duke and Duchess of York, but the waxwork that attracted the crowd, which it must be said had come from all corners of the world, was Benny Hill as Fred Scuttle. Children and adults clustered round the effigy giggling and taking endless photographs while Sylvester Stallone, Dolly Parton, and the former Miss Sarah Ferguson were ignored.

But there was always a gap between what the public saw and what his producers felt. The latter were always somewhat cagey about Benny Hill's performances – "Too many double entendres," said one executive. Some newspapers found him irresistible. As long ago as the early 1950s Moore Raymond in the *Sunday Dispatch* (a newspaper killed off not long afterwards) said, "He is positively the most original and refreshing comedian that British TV has discovered." Another paper described a TV performance as "an avalanche of laughs", but a slightly more quizzical note was struck by a Sunderland critic who, on Benny Hill's triumphant return to the theatre where, only a few short years before, he'd been given the bird but was now treated as a superstar, said, "Although we thought Benny Hill had a certain charm and was very amusing we did not think his material warranted cheers and claps every time he stopped to breathe."

This, however, is how the British public now saw Benny Hill, as a comic who could do no wrong. In the last analysis BBC Television went along with this, and for fifteen years he was one of their principal stars.

It took time though. His first show, in 1951, *Hi There*, was followed by *The Centre Show*, an outside broadcast from the forces rendezvous, the Nuffield Centre in Soho. After a tiff with the War Office, who suspected Benny of slipping in double entendres, the BBC shifted the programme to their Shepherd's Bush studio and renamed it *The Services Show*. In 1953 came *Show Case*, which at last gave Benny a chance to show the full range of his versatility. In 1955 he was rewarded with *The Benny Hill Show*, largely written by and starring Benny with guests Alma Cogan and Beryl Reid. It was, however, a flop.

In an article headed "Alas Poor Benny", one critic called the show "Ill-rehearsed" and commented, "He needs new scriptwriters with a keener edge to their humour." He even had a go at the supporting cast, saying, "His new dancing girls should go away and study precision dancing. Their voodoo effort was rather like a children's romp round a bonfire."

Hell's bells!

"Patchy ... lacked cohesion," said Clifford Davis of the *Daily Mirror*. Kenneth Bailey in the *People* said, "Benny ... had little new to offer," and his erstwhile fan Moore Raymond of the *Sunday Dispatch* commented, "*The Benny Hill Show* was nearly a flop. Benny wasted most of his talents on worthless stuff." Benny Hill was naturally enough rattled by these criticisms, but took heed and his next show was a vast improvement, gaining such criticisms as, "Here was Mr Hill in sparkling form."

The critics particularly enjoyed Benny Hill's parody of the panel game *Find the Link*, in which four panelists had to guess the element that the two contestants had in common.

In the sketch Jeremy Hawk played the Chairman and Benny Hill played the four panelists: Josephine Douglas, a presenter of the pop music show *6.5 Special*;

Moira Lister, the actress; Peter Noble, the film buff and later editor of *Screen International*; and Kenneth Horne, the businessman comedian well known in the 1950s for his many appearances on panel games.

Benny Hill used exactly the same technique as the original show – questioning the contestants in an attempt to find the link between them. The common factor was the absurd fact that both contestants had treacle in their left shoe.

By cutting from contestants to Benny Hill, first in the guise of Josephine Douglas, then as Moira Lister, Peter Noble, and Kenneth Horne, the effect was staggering and, in those primitive days before improved technology made such tricks easy to achieve, came across as a tour de force and something completely new.

The actual dialogue of the sketch was fairly basic and the jokes, such as they were, banal, but Benny in contrasting make-up and costumes – an effect attained by recording all the various sequences separately and then editing them together – was sensational. I think it is true to say that after this particular programme Benny Hill, as a TV performer, never looked back.

The negative reaction to his previous show had shaken him out of any complacency he might have had. In *Find the Link*, Benny Hill found his feet.

While this was happening on TV, radio was also after Benny's services. In 1954 he achieved the peak of radio success when he joined the cast of *Educating Archie* as Archie's new tutor.

Peter Brough, the ventriloquist, was a canny and astute businessman. As a

Find the Link: Josephine Douglas, Moira Lister, Peter Noble, Kenneth Horne

ventriloquist he wasn't in the super league, but observing the success of the American "vent", Edgar Bergen, who, with Charlie McCarthy, his smart talking dummy, and Mortimer Snurd, a foolish bumpkin, had been a big hit on American radio, he persuaded the BBC that they too could have a success with a radio ventriloquist.

Edgar Bergen had W. C. Fields among his supporting cast and Peter Brough saw that his show would be enhanced by the presence of the latest star to hit the headlines. Over the years he gave work to many, including Max Bygraves, Tony Hancock, Dick Emery, Beryl Reid, Robert Moreton, Bruce Forsyth, and Benny Hill. Mind you, Peter Brough needed all the support he could get, as comedian Jimmy Wheeler said of his ventriloquial skills, "Blimey, his mouth moves more than his dummy's does."

Eric Sykes, who wrote the show with Sid Colin, suggested many of the cast: Max Bygraves, Harry Secombe, Hattie Jacques (who he had seen in old-time music hall at the Players Theatre), Tony Hancock, and Robert Moreton. "But then other people came, not picked by me [says Sykes] including Beryl Reid. Now, I don't do jokes but Beryl would say to me, 'I've got this joke we could put in' and I didn't want jokes. So, there was a falling out. I felt invulnerable so I said 'Either she goes or I do.' And it was me who went. [So much for the invulnerability of script writers!] It was after I'd gone Benny Hill joined the show, so I don't really know what he did or how well he did it."

After Eric Sykes left (Sid Colin had gone too) the writers were Ronnie Wolfe and Eddie Maguire, who were very happy to write for Beryl Reid and Benny Hill. This is how they tackled it:

EDUCATING ARCHIE   1954
Script by EDDIE MAGUIRE AND RONALD WOLFE

BROUGH: The day before the wedding and no best man. Now, if only we could find someone to act as best man!

EFFECTS: DOOR OPENS

BENNY: Hello everyone!

ARCHIE: Mr Hill!

BENNY: That's me son – with me hair parted in the middle, and buttered on both sides!

BROUGH: Mr Hill – you're just the man I need. I'm looking for a best man for the wedding.

BENNY: Well don't look at *me* – I hate being best man. You stand there behind the happy couple – all on your jack, looking as though you've been knocked out in the semi-final.

ARCHIE: Now Mr Hill – come on – be a sport!

BENNY   Oh no, I'm against marriages. They're just like the three-ringed circus – engagement ring – wedding ring – and suffer-ring!

MRS B: But wouldn't you like to be married to a pretty girl?

BENNY: Get away. That's like jumping into the river because you're thirsty.

BROUGH: But what's your objection to being best man?

BENNY: Well, whenever I'm best man I get things all wrong. Last time they were tying things on the back of the car – they asked me for an old boot, and I brought the bride's mother.

MRS B: Was it a nice wedding?

BENNY: No, shocking. The bride's gown came down to the floor – that was *my* fault – I trod on the train! I was the worst best man ever.

ARCHIE: Now don't make excuses Mr Hill.

BENNY: But I *was*. I even forgot to order the cars, and at the last moment all I could get was a hearse – me and the bridegroom arrived at the church lying down.

BROUGH: I don't believe a word of it. Why are you trying to get out of it Mr Hill?

BENNY:	Well you can get into trouble at weddings. Why, only the other day I was talking to a couple of chaps, and one of these chaps, he said to me, this chap, he said, "Never be best man at a wedding" he said...
ARCHIE:	This chap?
BENNY:	This chap. He said it got him into a lot of trouble, he said.
ARCHIE:	This chap?
BENNY:	This chap. He said *he* was once best man, he said.
ARCHIE:	He said?
BENNY:	He said.
ARCHIE:	This chap?
BENNY:	This chap. He said, and that's what caused it, he said.
ARCHIE:	This chap.
BENNY:	This chap. He said the bridegroom punched him straight on the nose, he said.
ARCHIE:	He said?
BENNY:	He said.
ARCHIE:	This chap?
BENNY:	This chap. Just because he kissed the bride, he said.
ARCHIE:	But everybody kisses the bride.
BENNY:	I know, but this was the night before the wedding!

As with Frankie Howerd, Benny Hill's radio and TV fame led to offers of West End revue and in 1955 he starred with Tommy Cooper in a Bernard Delfont production, *Paris By Night*, which ran for a year at the Prince of Wales Theatre and yet was not considered a great success. Scantily-dressed showgirls were the big attraction of this *Folies Bergères* type production, but it wasn't long before the audiences were mainly foreigners in London on holiday for whom much of Benny Hill's stage material must have been a mystery.

In truth Benny Hill was never really at home in the theatre. That ego-shattering night in Sunderland must have made him extra cautious of the large spaces of theatres where the audience are at a distance and in the dark and can not be seen but only heard. For Benny television was the ideal medium and his rapport with the camera complete. On stage he appears to have been uneasy.

When, in the 1959 revue *Fine Fettle* at the Palace Theatre in London, he played twenty different characters, reaction was mixed. The critic of the *Daily Mirror* said, "It's very much a seaside show masquerading as a West End one."

Fine Fettle – "seaside stuff", said one critic

But Milton Shulman, in the *Evening Standard*, commented, "His cherubic face with its eyes fluttering like some berserk windscreen wiper represents, on the surface, the orthodox little man buffeted and baffled by fate. But he brings to this traditional comic characterisation a secret lip-smacking irreverence which gives his humour a boisterous, even bawdy quality."

Milton Shulman was right on target.

8 Sex and the Single Comedian

There are three ways in which a confirmed bachelor can live his life. One is to enter a monastery, or at any rate lead a completely (or comparatively) chaste life, another is to be heterosexually promiscuous, the third is to be gay.

Before we consider which of these paths the heroes of this book took in their lives, let us look again at the similarities in their backgrounds.

Both came from lower-middle-class families and both went to grammar school, leaving early because of their showbusiness ambitions. Each had one brother and one sister. Each had a domineering or bad-tempered father. On the other hand, both had loving mothers who clearly had more rapport with their talented sons than with their spouses. But that is where the similarity ends.

Frankie Howerd was, by his own account and the eye-witness of others, a nervy child and subject to tremendous emotional storms, seeking in religion solace and an outlet for his feelings of "difference", which the real world of suburban Eltham could not provide. In moments of crisis until quite late in his life he tended to "freeze", becoming incoherent and rudderless when faced with difficulties.

To see Frankie Howerd on stage when he was not in tune with his environment, his part, or his audience was to witness a man apparently without talent or timing. I know because in 1983 I adapted (at his request) Ben Jonson's *Volpone*, retitled *The Fly and The Fox*, in which, in spite of his enthusiasm during the rewriting – the "Howerding up" of the Jacobean classic – he was dreadful in the part of Mosca when it finally reached the stage. For one thing his performance lacked energy. If I had known that he was several years older than he admitted I might have understood. How different from his peak, in the 1940s, when he was humour and vigour personified, an electrifying performer.

I remember seeing him at the old Wood Green Empire thrilling a full house

LEFT Are you sure nobody will notice?

RIGHT Funny, I don't fancy any of them

with his tomfoolery. In one sequence he told the story of how his girlfriend, Deirdre Cuttlebunt – "what a pretty name," he'd say as an aside – had jilted him. "I went mad, I tell you, mad, [this was in the 1940s and I'm remembering some forty years on so please forgive any minor inaccuracies] so – I killed her. Yes! I hit her with my cricket bat. Now I'm consumed by remorse" – and pretending that the orchestra pit was a river, he'd continue – "That's why I've come here tonight. I'm going to throw myself in the river… I'm going to end it all." He would stagger melodramatically across the stage mumbling to himself until he reached the footlights and in an audible aside to the audience he'd refer to his ramble downstage and say, "It wasn't worth learning anything for that bit."

Then came the climax – a stentorian, "Shall I throw myself in the river? Shall I do it?" A stooge planted at the back of the stalls shouted "Yes!" "What, for you lot?" said Howerd, coming out of character, "Not bloody likely!" End of sketch.

Now, this was all larking about, but there's a lot of anger in it – and guilt too. The fact that there is a comic anticlimax suggests it has all been a huge joke, but I have come to suspect, the more I've thought about it, that behind the melancholy, the lack of self-confidence, the frequent, often self-induced bouts of professional failure which alongside the bluster and razzamatazz of Howerd's many successes made up this strange, quirky man's personality was guilt about his homosexuality. In many ways Frankie Howerd was intensely puritan, frowning on divorce and drunkenness, and a great frequenter of

churches for solitary vigils and silent prayer, but he was also an active homosexual, constantly seeking fresh male companions. His long and stable relationship with Dennis Heymer came when Frankie Howerd was well into middle age and (at least marginally) less promiscuous.

Many gays rejoice in their condition, and why not? We are not all created the same and it is ridiculous to suppose that everybody should behave in the same way. But Frankie discovered his own sexual propensities when homo-sexuality was not only disapproved of, but was a criminal offence which could lead the participants through the courts and into an all-male prison – that being the absurd foolishness of the notion of solving the problem of same-sex love. I often wonder what madman thought that locking up offenders in small cells, with two other men, for up to twenty-three hours a day would cure them of their sexual peccadillos. Fortunately the changes in the law which followed the publication of the Wolfenden Report in the late 1950s made relations between consenting adults in private legal and saved a great many people a great deal of anxiety.

As I have said, the cross that Howerd carried all his life was guilt. It may even have been the mainspring of his talent. It is possible that these emotional surges within him – desire followed by remorse – were the inward manifestations of what we have observed in his career: enormous success followed by almost total obscurity, followed in turn by great success.

With Benny Hill the impression is quite different. Here was a man who set his own course early on in life and pursued it unwaveringly until the end. In adult life he was a solitary man and yet he had men and women friends, smart, clever and sophisticated people with whom he felt as much at home as he did with the simple, the disabled and the disadvantaged.

Whilst Howerd's early urge was towards sainthood, Benny Hill's lifestyle was more in keeping with the priesthood than that of a showbusiness personality. He was frugal, cared nothing for money and appears to have had simple (even schoolboyish) sexual needs. There was a somewhat sleazy story printed in the *News of the World* in 1985 and recalled in John Smith's book about Benny.

Under the headline "I Was Benny Hill's Love Slave" a thirty-five-year-old actress and model confessed that nineteen years before, when she was sixteen, she met Benny who never laid a finger on her but said, "I'm going to show

Benny as Bunny
Funny, but it had been done before

you how to please me." The story continued, "And that's how it was for the next six years." A one-sided love affair indeed! On the other hand, if you'll excuse the expression, Sue Upton, one of the original Hill's Angels, said of the star, "He is the perfect gentleman … he always walks on the road side of the pavement. The height of good manners."

Leaving to one side the naivety of that last comment, Sue Upton's version of Benny Hill's love life seems to ring true more than the masturbatory fantasies recorded by the *News of the World*. Yet, if Benny Hill was not the "lewd capon", a description of him coined by a leading Hollywood writer, how did he get his kicks?

I think we find clues in his travels. In the course of his life and with so much leisure and no money worries he could and apparently did go everywhere, although certain places are highlighted: Hamburg, Marseilles, Bangkok and Tokyo, all of them noted for the number and ingenuity of the local ladies and gentlemen of easy virtue. Had he wished, Benny could have led a fully-extended sex life to the benefit of all concerned. Unless somebody tells us – and I'm not going to the Reeperbahn or the Ginza to find out – we'll never know for certain but, to quote again his comment, "In relations between the sexes the male is always disappointed", it doesn't seem as if he got much fun, adult fun that is, out of sex.

So, it appears that Frankie Howerd may have been a debauchee haunted by guilt, and Benny Hill the "perfect gentleman" who used brothels, but doubtless always said, "Thank you for having me," and gave a pound to the maid. But is it that simple?

Some psychologists see great significance in the early childhood of sexual deviants and when one looks closely at Benny Hill's birth and early childhood, certain facts emerge.

The first, which I am told is a significant feature of a child's earliest days, is when the mother has suffered depression prior to the birth. This was certainly true in the case of Benny's mother, whose postnatal depression, following the birth of her first, "ugly" son, Leonard, only abated with the birth of her second "pretty" son. From all accounts she was a loving mother who rarely, if ever, imposed discipline and was even possibly over-loving to her precious second son. The young Alfie reciprocated the cuddling affection, and sought it with a young girl friend when they were both five years old.

Later he was very much the pet of older girls and his brother tells a story of two of these girls fighting over him. He certainly had a sexual precocity not common among small boys.

Chased, but not chaste

His and her hose

In 1979, David Lewin, in a *Daily Mail* article about Benny Hill conquering American TV, we get another glimpse of the Hill view of sex. Remembering his early visits to the music hall, he said:

> When I was a lad it was always my ambition to be the principal
> comedian in touring revues.
>
> Those touring revues always had dolly birds in short skirts, frilly knickers
> and suspenders playing in sketches as maids and having to bend over to
> do the dusting, showing their black stocking tops.

As an adult at the height of his professional career much of his success came from dressing up as a woman, which apparently gave him great pleasure.

The number of wigs he used for his various impersonations was largely his quest for professional perfection but seems a little obsessive. According to one interviewer, in 1958, he was spending £1,200 a year on hiring or buying wigs. Benny commented: "The snag is most of the wigs are women's and it's spoiling

my love life. I think my female curls are scaring the girls away. They may think I'm a sissy."

Hill's obsession with wigs was not to the liking of one of his foremost allies in the press, Moore Raymond, who felt let down. As he wrote in an article in 1954:

> There I was going around telling myself and a lot of other people that Benny Hill was the most original, refreshing comedian that British TV has discovered. And what does B. Hill [sic] go and do to spoil it?
>
> He put on a blonde wig, evening dress, a coy tone to voice – and pretended to be a girl.
>
> The easiest and ugliest way for a comedian to get a laugh is to do a simpering female impersonation ... why did he resort to this distasteful style of humour?

Bypassing what were quite obviously Moore Raymond's hang-ups, I think we can go back to Benny's childhood for the answer.

His brother, Leonard, writes in *Saucy Boy*:

> Benny cannot remember the time when he was not sexually aware. He appears to have skipped latency, as the Freudians call the period when young boys have no interest in females. Attending Shirley Infants School in Wilton Road (Southampton) for the first time, at the age of five, he was delighted to find large numbers of girls held captive there [Now, I think that is a very strange phrase to use... I mean "captive"? – BT] His affection for them knew no bounds.

The headmistress was worried and his mother was sent for, but she was unconcerned:

> She felt that such interest as Alfie showed in the young doxies [An odd word to be used about five-year-old girls, as doxy is the archaic name for a prostitute. – BT] was quite natural... However, like the good mother she was, she advised her son not to be so full with his kisses.
>
> She, of course, was largely responsible for his extrovert behaviour. When we were infants she lavished her considerable maternal charms on her two sons with such abandon that neither of us had the slightest difficulty in recognising the opposite sex.

Streetcar named Desirée – from Benny's last show

Another youthful adventure had young Alfie in a narrow squeak with a child molester. Nothing happened, but when the lad recounted his experience all hell was let loose in the Hill household and the welter of threats, warnings and recriminations "taught Alfie one lesson – whatever happens, don't tell your parents".

I am neither knowledgeable about such things nor competent to express expert views on either infant or adult sexuality, but surely Leonard's descriptions lead inexorably to the conclusion that Benny Hill's adult attitudes to sex were formed in early life and, how can I put it – at his mother's knee? The pleasure he experienced then was never equalled.

In *Reveille*, 4 October 1969, Dennis Holman quoted Benny Hill's idea of a holiday:

> I would take £1,500 worth of travellers' cheques and jump on a plane and head for Hamburg. It is a beautiful city with a very happy night life.
>
> I would fly on to Paris. From there take the train to Marseilles. Go on to Barcelona, or on an impulse I might even hit Tokyo.
>
> I travelled light. Just the clothes I stood up in, a spare drip-dry shirt, pair of socks, and an overnight bag. I used to be quite tight-fisted.... Even when I could afford better it was hard to break from the habit of always going second class, never taking a taxi... Gradually I acquired a new set of values. Who was I hoarding it for?

Certainly at 1969 rates £1,500 for a holiday of a week or two seems anything but tight fisted.

In an excellent piece of reporting Dennis Holman covers a lot of ground, including a blow-by-blow account by Benny of being taken for a ride by a nightclub hostess. Expensive food, champagne, presents, tips etc. – and Hill concludes, "The bill is the equivalent of £80."

In my reckoning that still leaves £1,420 from the original £1,500, but the memory leads Hill to a bit of philosophy.

> It is life however and grist to my mill. It goes into my notebook. One day it may come in handy.

He then lets Holman into a little secret:

> The film *Baby Doll* gave me the idea for a sketch I do called Baby Boy in which I am kept in emotional subjugation by an overpowering wife and never allowed to grow up.

It must have been an unfortunate accident that Benny Hill never saw a sketch called "Eat Up Your Prunes", played first by Terry Scott in 1965, and in 1968 by Marty Feldman, in which a middle-aged man is kept in emotional subjugation by his mother. But, as they say, great minds think alike.

Eight years later, in 1977, in a Maureen Cleave interview in the London *Evening Standard*, the *Baby Doll* reversal is mentioned again, as are his visits to Marseilles.

In 1980, Howard Rosenberg of the *Los Angeles Times*, in an article for *TV Times* on the impact of Benny Hill in the United States, said:

> You could tell right off that Benny Hill wasn't Alistair Cooke.
>
> Maybe it was the wigs or the puffy pin cushion face. More likely it was the darting eyes. Hill looks like he'd goose his own grandmother.
>
> Sex – yes even cheap Benny Hill-type sex – has universal appeal...
> Hill's unlikely stylistic mix of Charlie Chaplin, Ernie Kovacs, and Milton Berle – the film speed ups, blackouts, visual gags, drag queening and cheap double entendres and bawdy songs emerge as a sort of polished drivel, a triumph of trash so revolting that unbelievably you tend to like it.

We are left, when the dust of conjecture has settled, with the facts of Howerd's constant untruths about girlfriends and indeed his invention of them when in fact none existed. His autobiography contains references to "taking a girlfriend to Paris" and similar situations, all of which to my certain knowledge are untrue. Compare that with Benny Hill's constant evasiveness about women: his politeness in their company, but no

Taste is a matter of opinion

95

She: "Infantile!"

He: "Ah, but what I'm thinking about isn't infantile."

recorded evidence of any sexual relationships. One is left to wonder what it really was that gave him sexual pleasure. Of Howerd there is no doubt, but I feel I've said enough about his sexuality, although there is undoubtedly more to know.

With Benny Hill the signals are fairly clear. He impersonated women at every opportunity, he was fascinated by the idea of being "a child held in emotional subjugation", and in a telling if ugly account of a TV warm-up, John Smith in *The Benny Hill Story* says: "Benny and director Dennis Kirkland get together for a quick sketch in which Benny plays the part of a woman on a crowded train and Kirkland is supposed to be a young man standing behind her. Kirkland's hand creeps round to grasp one of Benny's breasts and Benny, in a high-pitched voice, demands 'Young man, would you mind moving your hand?' Kirkland begins moving his hand in a sensuous, fondling movement and Benny lifts his eyes to Heaven in mock ecstasy, 'Mmmm, that's better'".

9 *Frankie Howerd – Back on top*

*I*n 1962 Frankie Howerd was "finished", so said the bosses of radio: Pat Hillyard, Jim Davidson and Con Mahoney; and of TV: Eric Maschwitz and Tom Sloan. The theatre people, principally impresario Leslie MacDonnell, who had taken over the reins at the London Palladium, felt that his star was on the wane and that it was time for new faces.

All three had to eat their words. By 1963 Frankie was a star again. But first there was the question of who managed his career. Once more the mysterious Stanley Dale moves into the picture. What happened to him?

I eventually got the full story from a number of sources and although I quote what I have been told, my informants wish to remain anonymous.

When Stanley Dale was last mentioned we had reached a stage in his career when he had discovered Frankie Howerd and had got him out of the clutches of Jack Payne, formed two companies; Frankie Howerd Ltd. and Frankie Howerd Scripts Ltd. (bringing in Eric Sykes), had signed up Jim Dale, and was putting out a number of variety bills on the music hall circuits. The acts he handled included singers (Tony Brent, Billie Anthony), speciality acts (wire walkers, dog acts, a man who made animals out of twisted balloons), and a comedian or two, including me – although I was in fact under contract to another agency, Fosters.

So far so good, but Stanley Dale was not all he seemed and informed opinion is that he "took Frankie Howerd and Eric Sykes to the cleaners". Another source said, "He was the biggest crook there ever was." Apparently he told the bank manager that he was putting money aside for Howerd and Sykes but that they mustn't be told because if either of them did get to know about it, they'd spend it. "You know how irresponsible these showbusiness people are. It'll be gone in a week."

This was rubbish, as both Howerd and Sykes were quite sensible in money matters, but the manager, taken in by Dale's plausible manner, said, "I won't mention a word, Mr Dale," and he didn't. Only after Dale had left the company, which was now called Associated London Scripts, did Howerd and Sykes realise that their money had gone with him.

The crunch actually came over the expenses of the skiffle group fronted by Jim Dale. When it made money Stanley Dale pocketed it, when it lost money the rest of the directors of ALS had to cough up the shortfall.

At last they said "Enough!" and told Stanley to go, but he produced a shrewd lawyer and in due course received a golden handshake of £5,000, no mean sum in the 1960s. With Stanley Dale gone, Associated London Scripts slimmed down, losing the variety acts and concentrating on writers and the two or three star performers on their books.

Now the agents handling Frankie Howerd's affairs were Roger Hancock and Beryl Vertue. Roger Hancock tried everything, but, as he admits, he was new to the business and found it difficult to persuade managements to use his client. He did get him a summer season at Yarmouth supporting Tommy Steele, and booked a few variety dates such as Chester and Crewe, Howerd sharing the billing with Peter Brough and Archie Andrews.

Pleasant though Crewe, Yarmouth and Chester undoubtedly are they aren't in the first rank of desirable dates, and Frankie Howerd wasn't at his happiest.

On 4 September 1961, Tom Sloan wrote to Roger Hancock:

> Dear Roger,
>
> Thank you for your letter dated 29th August concerning Frankie Howerd.
>
> I will certainly bear him in mind but I am afraid I have nothing to offer at the moment.
>
> Yours sincerely,
>
> (Tom Sloan)
> Assistant Head of Light Entertainment
> Television

Beryl Vertue had come to Associated London Scripts as a typist six years before, on 1 January 1955, at the suggestion of Alan Simpson with whom she had been to school. She saw nothing to object to and was soon happily rattling out fair copies of the Galton and Simpson, Eric Sykes, and Spike Milligan scripts. Gradually she became involved in vetting contracts and negotiating deals. Without realising it she had become an extremely efficient agent. A good brain and her native shrewdness made her see the simple logic of getting the

Alan Simpson and Ray Galton with Beryl Vertue (Ray's the one with the pipe)

right sort of deal for the clients of Associated London Scripts and although she denies it, she was, in fact, soon running the agency.

Faced with the Howerd problem she came up with a solution. If Frankie Howerd couldn't get work in the theatres why not try cabaret?

Although she says she was extremely suburban in her outlook in those days, she had heard about London's cabaret venues, Quaglino's, Esmerelda's Barn, the Jack of Clubs, and the Blue Angel, but she had never visited any of them. Picking the Blue Angel at random she looked in the telephone book for the number and, as she recalls, arranged an appointment with the owner, one Max Setty.

"I always thought night clubs were glamorous places. I'd never been in one – and I suppose they are glamorous at night, but at eleven o'clock in the morning it did look rather tatty. Anyway, I talked to the owner and he agreed to give Frank a date."

According to Beryl Vertue, Howerd wasn't keen on the idea of doing West End cabaret as he thought his material was too broad, but the people who went to night clubs like the Blue Angel were the same sort of people who went to variety theatres and listened to the radio.

From my own experience playing two weeks at the Blue Angel, I did exactly the same act as in previous weeks at music halls in Yorkshire, and afterwards

"I blame Galton and Simpson for this"

a lady came up to me and said, "Your material is much too sophisticated for them here."

Although he would deny it furiously, Frankie Howerd was at his best with a sophisticated audience and even during his lean years was always the hit of the evening at the annual *Evening Standard* Drama Awards.

In 1962 Frankie had more or less decided to give up show business and buy a pub, but at that year's *Evening Standard* Awards he was at his most sparkling – "The best actors here tonight are the losers," he quipped, "look at them smiling and clapping." Peter Cook, who with Alan Bennett, Dudley

Moore and Jonathan Miller had won a prize that year for *Beyond the Fringe*, thought that Frankie was wonderful and, totally unaware that he was on the verge of giving up the business, determined to get him for the recently opened Establishment Club, which, along with *Private Eye* magazine (which, incidentally, Cook also owned) and BBC TV's *That Was The Week That Was*, was riding on the crest of the satire boom.

Frankie, who was in pantomime in Southsea, duly finished his season and later in 1962 began his stint at the Blue Angel – the venue which had brought David Frost to the attention of Ned Sherrin, the producer of *TW3*, when he was looking for someone to act as anchor man for the new show. The spot had been intended for John Bird, but he had accepted an offer of work in New York.

Howerd's success at the Blue Angel restored some of his self esteem and when he was approached by Peter Cook to appear at the Establishment Club in Greek Street, Soho, he first said yes, but then panicked and according to Beryl wanted to cancel the booking. Beryl being Beryl said, "But you must do it. You promised."

Peter Cook confessed after their first meeting that he had needed a couple of stiff whiskies to nerve himself to ask Howerd to appear. Frank was equally on edge and said he also had needed a couple of large ones to agree to a meeting. Although Howerd was cautious about the reception he might get at the Establishment, eventually, stiffened by Beryl Vertue's resolve, he made his debut there and was a great success.

This is part of his act recorded at the Establishment:

FRANKIE HOWERD AT THE ESTABLISHMENT 1962
Script by Johnny Speight, Ray Galton and Alan Simpson

Er, brethren, before we start the eisteddfod I must apologise to you – well, no, it's not an apology it's an appeal, well, no it's an explanation: no, it's an apology. I'll tell you why because er – you see, ah, I'd like to explain how I happened to get here ... before we start – because as you know I'm a humble music hall comedian, a variety artist. I'm not usually associated with these sophisticated venues and I – no – well, a lot of people have said to me "I'm surprised at you going to a place like that". It's a bit different from a Granada tour with Billy Fury, and if I explain how I come to be here it might take the blame off me a bit, you understand. It might disarm criticism ... so you won't expect anything too sophisticated. Now, please – this is going to be a rowdy do, I can see that.

Ladies and gentlemen, you see, every year they have these drama awards at the Savoy – the *hotel*. There's a great many cafes with that name now, and they have dinner there and they give those drama awards … it's a good do – a good do and it's free – and every year I'm always asked to give a little speech – tell them a few jokes – I always look forward to this because it's the nearest thing I get to a West End appearance – a sort of annual pilgrimage to Mecca, and this particular year, this last year, I'd done my stint, my little bit, and I was standing outside afterwards in the foyer looking nonchalant and this young man came over to me; quite a presentable boy. He said "I'd like to introduce myself – I'm Cook". I said "oh, it was a lovely meal". He said "No, no, I'm Peter Cook". I said "I still enjoyed the meal" – then the penny dropped – He's the chap who runs this place or fronts for it or whatever it is he does. I don't know – I don't pry, I don't pry. I take my money at the end of the week and I go – after all whatever they do is their business – I wish to God it was mine, I tell you that. So, anyway, Peter Cook said – "We were all watching you tonight, all four, and we thought it was rather amusing". So I thought, oh … so I unbent as well. So he said, 'I was wondering if you'd do a season at the Establishment". "Well", I said … "well I … er", I thought if I stuttered long enough he might mention money. The lips were pursed… I've often been asked to do a tour or work a week somewhere, or even stand up and give a turn but I'd never been asked to do a *season* anywhere so I thought ooh, I might be another Joyce Grenfell.

… So, anyway, ladies and gentlemen, I've got nothing against this place. Admittedly you meet some odd people here but not that I pry, as I say I keep myself to myself. I think it's best. I mean, you don't get into any mischief do you – unfortunately…

(*he asks politely*) Would you mind if I sat down? After all I'm not loping around like Jonathan Miller. Besides, for the money they're paying me I should be dynamic.

So, listen, I was talking to this Peter Cook boy – very clever – all those boys are – Beyond The Fringe … very clever those boys. I think they should turn professional. They tell me now they've learned to put on make up. Soon they're going to use it on the stage.

So, I was talking to Peter Cook. That's the one who does it full time, and he said, "When you open here at the Stabbers what are you going to do? What material are you going to work?" That's a word he's picked up – work…

There's much more in the same vein until the subject of satire is broached and Cook is alleged to urge him to attack the Government. Howerd responds:

> The Government, the Civil Service, but they're your audience here, they think it's rather sweet. Let's face it the whole place is only a snob's *Workers' Playtime*. Instead of making jokes about the foreman we make jokes about Harold Macmillan – it's the same thing.
>
> He's such an easy target – it's just one man against the Government. Admittedly I think he's silly to himself. His public image – let's face it, he's no Bruce Forsyth. I've had no dealings with the man. I say no dealings ... there was this little fracas we had about the Common Market ... and I thought, if you want to find something out go to the top man. Right, so he was down at Chequers – lovely place, it goes with the job – that's why he's hanging on to it. Now, I was out on a cycle rally and we were passing by Chequers – I thought, I'll nip in. I'm sorry – I told him. I was very forthright, stupid to be anything else. I said, "Harold, be careful". I said, "Harold, don't rush into this, I beg you". I don't think he got the message. Well, it's very difficult when you're shouting through a letter box.

There is more political stuff and Frankie concludes his act with a joke:

> This woman ... married ten years, and in those ten years her husband said three words to her. Damn shame. Three words in ten years. Why, it's ridiculous. She got the divorce and the custody of the three children.

Does that last joke sound familiar? Yes, Benny Hill did a variation on it, which I quoted in the opening chapter.

At first Johnny Speight was very suspicious of everyone at Associated London Scripts. He had been introduced to the incumbents by Frankie Howerd, and having been made aware of Howard's sexual peccadillos, suspected the rest of them as being similarly inclined.

They weren't, of course, as Johnny quickly found out and equally quickly he learned the trade of comedy scriptwriting. He brought a new aspect to Howerd's work – political humour. In 1963 this was apt as the country was becoming bored with the Conservatives, who had been in government for a dozen years. It was time for a change.

Jokes about Harold Macmillan were lapped up by audiences everywhere. Ned Sherrin spotted in Howerd at the Establishment an ideal special guest for

A bedtime story from BBC producer Alastair Scott Johnston

TW3: "I thought, if he can do an hour at the Establishment he could certainly do fifteen minutes on national television."

Sherrin also noticed the key to Howerd's appeal, or perhaps it would be fairer to say the appeal which Johnny Speight had written into his act: "Reducing international politics to kitchen conversation." So, Frankie Howerd did his stuff on *That Was The Week That Was* and was a sensational success.

Suddenly the man who was finished was a star again and everyone rushed to secure his services. The thoughts of retirement to a country pub vanished and the reality of renewed fame (and fortune) took its place. However, Howerd never forgot how much he owed his scriptwriters. From the beginning he knew that a top-line performer was as good as his material, and his decline had been caused in part by rotten scripts.

Eric Sykes reckons that if Frankie Howerd could have had his way, "he would have grabbed all the writers in the country and locked them in a shed and said, 'I've got a *Workers' Playtime* next week – write me a script.'"

In a great many cases, whoever wrote Frankie's scripts, he would take them to Eric Sykes for his approval, and Laurence Marks and Maurice Gran, who wrote for Howerd in the 1970s, claimed that whenever he acquired new writers he would ask the previous writers to vet their scripts.

This was news to me, but during my researches I came upon some correspondence. I was writing solo for Frankie (1961) and these letters explain the situation. I had been asked by him for some scripts for a short radio series and in all innocence thought I was the only writer involved. I duly posted copies to Frankie Howerd at the theatre in Yarmouth where he was playing, and further copies to the producer, Alastair Scott Johnston at the BBC. However, clearly, in the meantime Howerd had also approached Bob Monkhouse and Denis Goodwin for other scripts on the same subjects.

This was at a time, remember, when he was finding it difficult to get work, and when very few producers and writers had faith in him and he'd acquired a reputation for being difficult. He never told me about the Monkhouse/Goodwin connection. Small wonder that people tended to lose patience with him. Not that my scripts didn't need improving, but it was disappointing not to know what was being done. Anyway, here is the correspondence:

Frankie Howerd Esq.,   12 September 1961
Windmill Theatre,
Great Yarmouth.

Dear Frank,

    You will be happy to know that both your scripts are nearing completion, and I promise you that they will be in the post tomorrow, Wednesday. That means that you will receive them on Thursday, which should give you ample time to tear them up and make other arrangements by the time you go on holiday. (That is a joke. At least I hope so!)

    Warmest regards,

Yours sincerely,
(Barry Took)

Alastair Scott Johnston, Esq.,   27 September 1961
Aeolian Hall,
New Bond Street,
London W.1.

Dear Alastair,

    Herewith scripts for Frankie Howerd for his first two programmes.

    Undoubtedly these will be changed and re-written, but I have not been able to contact Frankie, so am sending you the basic scripts for your OK.

Yours sincerely,
(Barry Took)

Frankie Howerd, Esq.,

19 Napier Place,

W.14.   19th September 1961

Dear Frank,

I don't quite know what to suggest for Sunday's script. I think
either of the two versions of the sculpture lecture will give you a good
performance and relate to what will follow in future weeks, so that disposes
of the spare.

Of the two sculpture versions the Barry Took is, I would have
thought, the cleverer and gives you, with minor amendments, more chance
to do a performing performance, if you understand me. And in view of
the musical content of the programme the audience is likely to be more
rather than less intelligent. The Monkhouse/Goodwin is more on a plate.
It's more an "act" and the other is more material for an "appearance", and
I have a feeling it will accord better with what our particular audience
would like from you.

I suggest therefore that if you are happy about it, why not take
the basis of the Barry Took and put in some of the Monkhouse/Goodwin
lines, but don't destroy the original flavour?

Can you bring copies of the final result to the studio? I shall look
forward to seeing you about 1.30 or so.

Hope you had a good time in Venice.

Regards,

Sincerely,

(Alastair Scott Johnston)

I can't locate a copy of the Sculpture monologue but here is a snatch of the
sort of thing I was writing for Howerd in 1961.

FRANKIE HOWERD SCRIPT FOR VARIETY PLAYHOUSE
Script by Barry Took

Ladies and Gentlemen – I stand before you tonight on the threshold of
the New Year – with the bright promise of the future refulgent with
hope, and say to you – Oh, these garters do bind. No – no, well they do.
My legs will look like trellis work when I get my socks off. Yes. Oh, I

wish Deirdre wouldn't keep giving me garters for Christmas. Every January I go through agony – How can I think about the bright promise of the future with my legs all mottled. Well, it could be worse – I mean there's no fun in mottled legs but at least it takes my mind off my real worries.

Yes, missus, I have got worries. I can see you saying to yourselves, "What has 'e got to worry about?" "He don't look a worry guts!" I know to look at me you wouldn't think I had the world's worries on my shoulders – or mottled legs. But I have both. Pity poor Francis all mottled and melancholy.

It's my own fault. I'm silly to myself. I was in this chemist's you see...

After that came a long, rambling anecdote about acquiring a free ballpoint pen with a bar of soap, a routine which worked reasonably well.

Among the many writers helping him out was Johnny Speight, one of whose inventions went something like, "It's not easy to be a comedian. Some do it by wearing funny clothes, some comedians have a funny face. Me? I have this curse of beauty.'

Anything more absurd than Frankie Howerd saying he was cursed with beauty is hard to imagine and it was a line he used frequently with great effect. With Speight, as with most people he got to know and like, Frankie Howerd would not hesitate to invite himself and his sister Betty to dinner.

He once chided Speight for never asking them to the Speights' home, so Johnny said, "Alright, let's make a date. Come round next Thursday at eight o'clock." Speight said, "I completely forgot. I was at home the next Thursday, in the front room reading a book. I looked up and there, walking up to the front door were Frank and Betty. I said to my wife, 'Oh God, I forgot to tell you. I've invited them to dinner. What can you give them?' My wife said, 'We've only got bacon and eggs in the house.' I said, 'OK, give them that,' and that's what we had for our evening meal. Frank's reaction was indignant. He said, 'You invited us to dinner. This isn't dinner it's *breakfast*'."

Soon after the *TW3* breakthrough came the possibility of a very big deal, the lead in the London version of the American musical, *A Funny Thing Happened On The Way To The Forum.*

It seems that he had been suggested by John Gielgud. The producers, Richard Pilbrow and Hal Prince, agreed and sent the authors of the show, Burt Shevelove and Larry Gelbart, to see Frankie Howerd at work. Work at that moment was playing in *Puss In Boots* at the Coventry Hippodrome. Not surprisingly Howerd was petrified at the thought of what these two sophisticated

En route to the top via the Manchester Opera House

What a funny woman! Frankie with Kenneth Connor in
A Funny Thing Happened On The Way To The Forum

Pseudolos (Frankie Howerd) meets Pseudolos (Zero Mostel)

New Yorkers would make of a provincial British panto. As it turned out they loved it, became great fans of Howerd, and were delighted that he was going to play Pseudolos, the slave who dominates the action, who had been played in New York by Zero Mostel. Rehearsals began in August 1963 under the stern control of the director George Abbott. Howerd in his autobiography says of Abbott: "He had his problems. We were a British cast with styles, voices, mannerisms and methods known by British audiences, but none of which meant anything to Abbott." The cast included Jon Pertwee, Kenneth Connor, "Monsewer" Eddie Gray, and Robertson Hare, as motley a group of individualists as you could crowd into one production. However, the mix worked and George Abbott returned to the States, saying to the cast before opening night, "You've all worked very hard, but I think you'll get controversial notices. Half the press will like it, the other half will hate it... I'm off to America now."

Off he went and left them to it. In fact the show was a tremendous hit and the critics were almost entirely unanimous in their praise. *Forum* ran until July 1965 – Frankie's comeback was complete.

10 *Film fun and stage success*

While Benny Hill could be said to have made his name on television and Frankie Howerd was first and foremost a radio star, both made many stage appearances and appeared in several films. Never together let it be said and, with rare exceptions, little success on the big screen.

In 1956 Benny Hill starred in a film called *Who Done It?* written by T. E. B. Clarke and directed by Basil Dearden. Benny's reaction in later years gives a glimpse of his view of his movie debut. When told by a reporter that *Who*

Benny with David Kossoff in *Who Done It?*

Benny as a lovable old toymaker in *Chitty Chitty Bang Bang* –
"A pleasure," said critic Shaun Usher

Done It? was to be shown on television, Benny said, "In that case I'm taking the next plane to Marseilles."

His next film, in 1959, was *Light Up The Sky* in which he co-starred with Tommy Steele as a music hall double act who get called up in world war II and are stationed on a searchlight battery. In 1965 he had a cameo role in *Those Magnificent Men In Their Flying Machines*, as the chief of the local fire brigade. Then in 1968 came another cameo role in *Chitty Chitty Bang Bang*, as a loveable German toymaker.

Shaun Usher, the experienced film critic, remembers Benny's role in the film with pleasure and says he is surprised that Benny did very little film work after that. In fact, as far as I can discover Benny Hill only appeared in one other film, *The Italian Job*, made in 1969 and starring Michael Caine and Noël Coward.

In 1969 Benny Hill's career move from the BBC to the ITV company Thames (via two "specials" for ATV, destined for sale to the USA and which

Benny hated) was part of his general desire for new challenges. Under the headline "Benny Hill Heading In A New Direction – Behind The Camera", Shaun Usher wrote:

> Brothers, let me present a new union member – Benny Hill… Benny is now a card-carrying member of the Association of Cinematograph Television and Allied Technicians.
>
> Why? "This means I can work as a director occasionally on shows I have written myself." Unfortunately Mr Hill's union card came through just too late for him to direct *Eddie in August* [a silent comedy that Hill had devised himself].

Peter Black reviewed the film, on 4 June 1970, in the *Daily Mail*:

> I wish I could say that Benny Hill's half hour silent comedy, *Eddie in August* (Thames TV), was the funniest thing since *City Lights*, but I can't get the words out.
>
> Benny made this little movie with co-producer John Robins last summer.
>
> The theme was his usual one, presenting himself as the frustrated chaser of girls.
>
> He was always after the same pretty one, but she went off with the handsome chap, and always left Benny with her plain friend.
>
> He bought a dog (joke about the dog making water over his foot) and an old car (joke about it breaking down) to impress her.
>
> He went into dream sequences in which things went better; in one long convoluted one he was a surgeon giving an old car a transplant. But it was symptomatic of the film's lack of any really worked-out central idea that even in some of his dreams he was the loser.
>
> The studio audience, which has always included that woman with a fat, contented bray who is worth £20,000 a year to Thames TV, laughed quite a lot. But it did nothing to advance Benny's name.
>
> He really must drop this character he has created for himself. The one thing that a baffled amorist is not is funny; and there was something in Benny's performance of following girls about, ogling at them, crouching on the grass to get a better look up their legs, that was much sadder than he seemed to realise.
>
> The character has become a ball and chain to his art.

After *Eddie* Benny went back to his usual style of TV programmes and never made another movie.

"How about some nice veg – for your hat?"
Frankie in a cameo in *The Ladykillers* with Katie Johnson

Howerd in flight in *The Great St Trinian's Train Robbery*

Nor was Frankie Howerd's film career particularly glittering, although it was rather more extensive. His first film, and possibly his best, was the 1953 Val Guest comedy thriller, *The Runaway Bus*. Frankie played the driver who managed to get lost in the fog. The film had such a small budget it was "shot mainly in the fog to save money on sets," he said.

In 1955 came a small part in the comedy *An Alligator Named Daisy*, then another "animal" picture, *Jumping For Joy*, about greyhound racing. His cameo role in *The Ladykillers*, an Ealing comedy, the same year was short but effective. In 1956 he made *A Touch Of The Sun*, with Dennis Price, Alfie Bass and Bill Fraser, which Leslie Halliwell in his *Film Guide* pronounced "limp".

I've already mentioned the 1958 flop, *Further Up the Creek*, but for poor Frankie worse was to follow. In 1962 he played KoKo in *The Cool Mikado*, a "with it" version of the old Gilbert and Sullivan warhorse. The producer,

director and writer was the then unknown Michael Winner, whose lack of taste is only equalled by his vast conceit. According to Howerd Winner's first words to him were, "You must understand that I'm a genius." He went on, "Who makes your suits? The one you're wearing is very badly made. That's what makes you look so fat." Winner may well have known something about suits, but in those days he didn't know anything about movies and *The Cool Mikado* was a mess and received a very bad press.

Howerd's verdict on the finished picture: "It had the appearance of being made in a wind tunnel. Nobody could make any sense of it and I can say without equivocation that not only was it the worst film ever made but the one production in showbusiness that I'm positively ashamed to have appeared in ... it was absolutely incomprehensible gibberish."

After that experience I suppose anything would have seemed an improvement, but apart from a tiny role in *The Fast Lady*, a vehicle for Leslie Phillips, his next decent film was the 1965 *The Great St Trinian's Train Robbery*. By then he was a box office draw again and the film made money.

There followed appearances in two *Carry On* films, *Carry On Doctor* and *Carry On Up The Jungle*, a cinema film of his TV success *Up Pompeii* (a vulgar, unfunny version of what had been a very popular series) and then, for Ned Sherrin, *Up The Chastity Belt* set at the time of Crusades, and *Up The Front* set in world war I.

Next came *The House In Nightmare Park* (1973), with Ray Milland, a small

Frankie with Ray Milland

OPPOSITE *Up The Front*

part in the Robert Stigwood production *Sergeant Pepper's Lonely Hearts Club Band*, and two more Gilbert and Sullivan operas, *HMS Pinafore* and *Trial By Jury*.

In the theatre Frankie Howerd was more successful, particularly in glossy West End revues, such as Bernard Delfont's *Pardon My French* at the Prince of Wales in 1953. His 1955–6 ventures, *Charley's Aunt* and *Tons of Money*, were also hits, although *A Funny Thing Happened On The Way To The Forum* was his biggest. I really think though that his favourite stage show was the 1966 Delfont spectacular, *Way Out In Piccadilly*, at the Prince of Wales theatre, well written by Galton and Simpson and Johnny Speight, and directed by Eric Sykes. It ran for four hundred and eight performances. Frankie and Cilla Black, his co-star, really enjoyed working together, became friends and remained so from then on.

This success led to Frankie being invited yet again by Bernard Delfont to appear in that year's Royal Variety Show. After typical Howerd hesitation he agreed. In fact he appeared in seven Royal Variety Shows (1950, 1953, 1961, 1966, 1968, 1969, 1978) and also entertained the Royal Family at Windsor.

A pat on the head for Bernard Delfont

With his favourite co-star Cilla Black

Perhaps Howerd's strangest theatrical venture was in 1968 in a production of a play called *The Wind In The Sassafras Tree* by the French playwright, René de Obaldia, with the English version adapted by Galton and Simpson. It was a send-up of all mid-western American dramas and Frankie Howerd played "a Kansas dirt farmer".

The try-out was at the Belgrade Theatre, Coventry and according to Alan Simpson it was greeted with acclamation by the Coventry audiences. "A triumph," he said, "the best reaction to anything Ray and I wrote for the stage." It had some difficulties in rehearsal when the finale of the first act seemed to be creating problems, and act two started uncomfortably. Howerd's manager, Dennis Heymer, suggested that they split it into three acts rather than two, which they did, and the problem was solved.

The show was clearly a resounding success and although the French author was astonished by some of the things Alan Simpson and Ray Galton had done to his original play, it worked very well for the English audiences who packed the theatre every night. But the Howerd nerves took over again and Frankie felt very insecure about a London opening, remembering his earlier flop with *Mr Venus*.

That problem was solved when the American director of the show, Arthur Lewis, said, "Why go to London at all? Why not come direct to America?" It seemed the perfect solution, but the play struck the trouble that besets many American shows, cuts and rewrites on the road. On top of that it received a very bad press in Boston and the management panicked, ordering more rewrites and changing the title to *Rockerfeller and the Red Indians*. In Washington the show was a hit and received rave reviews, but in New York the critics, particularly Clive Barnes, then the most influential of them all, panned the show and the producer, David Merrick, pulled it off after a week. In November 1968, the unhappy Howerd returned to England.

The Wind in the Sassafras Tree – a hit in Coventry; a flop in Boston, Mass.

11 *1969 – Up Pompeii*

*I*n the summer of 1969, I was approached by Tom Sloan and asked if I'd care to become Advisor to BBC TV's Comedy Department, working under the Head of Comedy, Michael Mills. I agreed, and Mills and I surveyed our small but important empire.

There wasn't much to see. A series called *Broaden Your Mind*, starring Tim Brooke-Taylor and Graeme Garden was pleasant, but not earth shattering, and an alleged sit. com. starring Tessie O'Shea wasn't even pleasant. We set to work to try and improve things.

Ned Sherrin offered a series, written by N. F. Simpson, called *World In Ferment*, which we bought. I went to work to pull together the cast of what became *Monty Python's Flying Circus*, and I persuaded Mills to give Barry Humphries a special (his first in the UK) in the hope that it could be developed into a series. It was, but the series was not a world beater.

What we really needed was a knock-down, drag out, broad, farcical comedy, and one day Michael Mills swept into my office, slapped a script onto my desk and said, "What do you make of that?" It was called *Up Pompeii* and was written by Talbot Rothwell, the best of the "Carry On" writers. I read it, roared with laughter and said to Mills, "It's extremely dirty, but extremely funny. It's bound to be a hit."

Mills, describing how he came upon the idea, in a 1987 edition of the radio programme, *Kaleidoscope*, said, "I was on holiday with Tom Sloan and we visited Pompeii. We wandered away from the main part of Pompeii to where the little shops and bordellos had been and suddenly I said to Tom, "It's amazing. I expect to see Frankie Howerd come loping round the corner," and Tom said, "why not?" Frankie Howerd's success in *Forum* had not gone unnoticed by Sloan and "the man is finished" was completely forgotten.

Mills continued, "So, I got a copy of the plays of Plautus – in English, and sent them to Tolly Rothwell with a note: What about this for Frankie Howerd? Rothwell liked the idea. As Mills said, "Many of the plays of Plautus (like

Forum) are based on this cunning slave who is running everything in a family, to his own advantage."

Talbot Rothwell wrote a script, Frankie Howerd read it and liked it. "I laughed out loud," he said, "very rare for me. *Up Pompeii* seemed to me to contain the basic ingredients of popular British humour: cheeky, cheerful, seaside postcard bawdiness, designed for a relaxed belly laugh." Which, I suppose, is another way of saying what I said to Michael Mills – "It's extremely dirty but extremely funny."

Frankie was a little worried. He wrote in his autobiography, "I said to the BBC can we get away with it? Is it going too far for the small screen?" The answer was "Don't worry," and he agreed to make a pilot to see what the public reaction would be. The pilot was a success and the series was duly made.

The bill matter in *Radio Times*, announcing the pilot programme, called *Up Pompeii* "a sort of 'Carry On up the Forum'", which describes it to perfection. Indeed that was what it was supposed to be and it gave the BBC the broad comedy it so badly needed.

Howerd in a radio interview some years later said, "in a way it was a very moral show because here was a family being naughty but nobody ever did anything" and, in fact, the *Catholic Herald* agreed that it was "very moral".

Here is a sample of the script recorded on 4 July 1969.

FADE UP

A STREET IN POMPEII

(OUTSIDE THE HOUSE OF LUDICRUS SEXTUS, THE WELL-KNOWN
SENATOR)

(A FEW CITIZENS CROSS, CHATTING)

(AS THEY CLEAR, LURCIO COMES OUT OF THE HOUSE, CARRYING A
BROOM AND OTHER CLEANING UTENSILS. HE IS DRESSED AS A SLAVE.
SUDDENLY APPEARS TO NOTICE THE AUDIENCE AND SPEAKS DIRECTLY
INTO CAMERA)

LURCIO

Oh hello, are you here already? I didn't realise it was that late.

(HE BRINGS OUT A LARGISH "FOB" WATCH AND LOOKS AT IT.
C. S. WATCH. IT IS A MINIATURE SUNDIAL WITH ROMAN NUMERALS)

LURCIO

Oh dear, oh dear, how tempus fugits! Ah well, on with the drama and
off with the clobber.

(HE CHUCKS ALL THE CLEANING THINGS TO ONE SIDE AND BOWS TO
THE AUDIENCE IN TRADITIONAL STYLE)

LURCIO

Greetings, noble citizens, simple plebians, crafty artisans and arty
courtesans. I think that about covers the lot. The bit I am about to do
now is called the prologue, which is not only a quick way of getting to
the fruity part of the plot, but also fills you in on … who's who, who
does what to who, to whom they does what to, not to mention how.

The prologue – *Up Pompeii*

Which brings us back to the fruity part. To begin with, my name's Lurcio
and I'm a slave in the house of Ludicrus Sextus, which, to avoid
disappointment, means Ludicrus the Sixth – *not* the Sexy. Well, he's a
senator, you see, and politicians don't really have time for that sort of
thing. Well, not in *these* days they didn't.

LUDICRUS (OFF)

Lurcio! Where are you, Lurcio?

LURCIO

I'm out here, Master. That's him now. Probably lost his laurel leaves, the
old fool. Take no notice. As I was saying…

(LUDICRUS, IN SENATORIAL GARB, BUT WITHOUT LAUREL LEAVES,
DODDERS OUT OF THE HOUSE)

LUDICRUS

Lurcio, what are you doing out here?

LURCIO
I'm doing the prologue.

LUDICRUS
Oh, I beg your pardon. Try and make it quick, will you? I can't find my laurel leaves.

LURCIO
You'll have to get some fresh ones. The others had got greenfly.

LUDICRUS
(GOING BACK IN GRUMBLING) Oh jumping Jupiter. I hate them straight off the bush. Always brings me out in a rash...

LURCIO
Marvellous, isn't it? They can't do a thing without me, you know. Indispensable. That's why they made me the major domo of the household. I said *domo*. Well, I don't want any misunderstanding this early on. To proceed with the prologue. Our story takes place here, in ancient Pompey, which is situated just about ... let's see, how can I describe it? Well, if you think of Italy as the whole of a woman's leg, Pompey's not high enough up to be interesting. Anyway, as I was saying...
(CASSANDRA, AN ELDERLY PROPHETESS, DRESSED IN SOMBRE RAGS, ENTERS, WAILING)

CASSANDRA
Oh Pompeii!! Oh woe, woe and thrice woe!

LURCIO
Oh dear, it's her. Cassandra, an elderly prophetess dressed in sombre rags.

CASSANDRA
Hear my words, o wicked citizens of Pompeii!

LURCIO
We're going to get the death and destruction bit now.

CASSANDRA
Oh! I see a great fall. Your proud city will vanish in the sands of time!

LURCIO
What did I tell you? Oh, she does go on so.

CASSANDRA
Repent before it is too late!
Give up your evil and licentious ways!
(KNEELS DOWN AND STARTS THROWING DIRT OVER HER HEAD)

"This is Cassandra. You wouldn't think to look at her she once had a good job as a vestal virgin" – Frankie in *Up Pompeii*

LURCIO

And that's the ashes in the hair bit. Silly old bag. You'd never believe it to look at her, but she once had a good job as a vestral virgin. Yes, true. Then she went and lost it. Well, they do tend to, don't they? Yes. Poor old thing. Now all she's good for is a bit of sooth-saying.

CASSANDRA

(IN A WAIL) Soof, soof, soof, soof!

LURCIO

Oh yes, I knew that was coming. (HE STARTS CHIVVYING HER OFF) All right, dear, that's enough. Go and do it in the next street, there's a dear. Give them a treat. (HE SEES HER OFF AND TURNS BACK TO CAMERA) She can't help it, you know. She's at the funny time of life. Difficult. And mind you, she has a point about Pompey. Shocking things go on here. You wouldn't believe it! Licentiousness! Libertinage. Orgies! (LOOKS ROUND CAUTIOUSLY, THEN CONFIDENTIALLY) Even bingo. Oh yes. Up

"They can't do a thing without me you know" – *Up Pompeii*

in Rome they just do what the Romans do. But here they do the lot. Anyway, to get back to the prologue...

LUDICRUS COMES OUT OF THE HOUSE, WEARING LAUREL LEAVES AND CARRYING BATON OF OFFICE AND A SCROLL)

LUDICRUS

Lurcio, haven't you finished yet?

LURCIO

I've hardly started!

LUDICRUS

Well, I can't wait any longer. I have a speech to deliver in the senate.

LURCIO

(To CAMERA) And the best of Pompey luck to them.

LUDICRUS

It's my new bill proposing that slaves be given the right to purchase their freedom. I'd like you to hear it.

LURCIO

I was afraid you would.

LUDICRUS

(reading from scroll) Listen. Friends, Romans, countrymen, lend me your feet. I wish to...

LURCIO

Just a minute. Lend me your *feet?*

LUDICRUS

Yes. Don't you like it?

LURCIO

If I may suggest, Master ... why not lend me your ears?

LUDICRUS

Ears? But that wouldn't make sense. You see, I go on ... help me to stamp out the curse of slavery, and you can't stamp anything out with your ears, can you? One must be *rational.*

LURCIO

Oh yes! If we're going to be rational, exactly what do we purchase our freedom with?

LUDICRUS

Money of course. I thought – five hundred drachmas.

LURCIO

How do we save five hundred drachmas when you don't pay us anything?

LUDICRUS

Oh well, that's your problem.

LURCIO

I see.

LUDICRUS

I can't do *everything* for you.

(EROTICA COMES RUNNING OUT OF THE HOUSE. A PRETTY FLUFFY LITTLE THING OF ABOUT EIGHTEEN)

EROTICA

Pater. Oh there you are. Pater darling, can I have the chariot today please?

LUDICRUS

Oh well, I was going to use it myself.

EROTICA

Oh please, darling. I want to drive out to the elysian fields and pick mater some flowers.

(LURCIO SPEAKS TO CAMERA)

LURCIO

That's his daughter Erotica. I could tell you things about her. Oh yes ... what? One of the original libertine-agers! Oh yes. Don't let that stuff about flowers for mater fool you. She meets a young gladiator out there. And, believe me, they'll flatten more flowers than they'll pick.

(LUDICRUS HAS BEEN SEARCHING THROUGH HIS CLOTHING FOR KEY TO CHARIOT. FINDS IT)

LUDICRUS

There you are, my dear.

EROTICA

Oh thank you, darling Pater! (KISSES HIM AND RUNS OFF).

LUDICRUS

(LOOKS AFTER HER FONDLY) Dear child. So delightfully chaste.

LURCIO

Yes, and so easily caught.

In the end they only made two series of *Up Pompeii* (fourteen programmes in all). Frankie felt that it was getting repetitive, but both series were repeated and got even bigger viewing figures than the original transmissions, a common factor in programme scheduling, particularly with a popular show.

In 1972 the BBC asked for another series of *Up Pompeii*, but by then Talbot Rothwell, who had been writing in association with Sid Colin, was involved with *Carry On* films and his health was not of the best. It was a sad loss when he died, in February 1981 aged 64, at a hospital in Worthing where he had been admitted with a heart condition. So a variation on the theme was devised, in which Frankie Howerd appeared as a guard in a harem, and the series was called *Whoops Baghdad*. It didn't really amount to much. Although well produced by John Howard Davies, it suffered from having several writers and the quality varied from episode to episode. Nor did John Howard Davies find Frankie Howerd the easiest person to work with.

He was particularly difficult about the scripts. He'd hate things that John Howard Davies found funny and loved scenes that John didn't think worked.

"She was big – almost to a fault" – Frankie in *Whoops Baghdad*

He worried about everything from the decor (too good) to the cast (not good enough) but curiously in some cases preferred a bad actress to a good one. I guess that one of Frankie Howerd's "tricks" was to say, after a scene, in an aside to the audience, "*She* was dreadful!"

In 1991 London Weekend Television recorded a "one off", a sort of update of *Up Pompeii*, called *Further Up Pompeii*. By now, twenty years after the original series, things had changed.

In the plot Lurcio (Howerd) was no longer a slave but had been granted his freedom in his late Master's will. In fact he had forged the entry and the villain of the piece had found out and was blackmailing him. The programme, though lavishly mounted and well written by Paul Minett and Brian Leveson, had problems – most of them to do with Frankie Howerd.

For one thing he was seventy-four years old and very fat so that the short toga of the earlier series was out of the question. The costume they gave him was unsuitable and, as Eric Sykes, and Galton and Simpson would agree, Frankie was never a good mover. Also, as at seventy-four you tend to move more slowly, moving slowly *and* clumsily does not help comedy.

A worse fault was that (at Howerd's insistence) it was shot without an audience. (An audience was shown the film at a later date and its laughter dubbed on, which sounded artificial and was unsynchronised). When on the dress rehearsal the many technicians present laughed uproariously at the show, Frankie realised his mistake and asked for a studio audience. But it was too late. The size of the set left no room for one.

Minett and Leveson noted the Howerd trick I mentioned earlier when, after one actor's exit, he ad libbed to camera, "Shocking actor isn't he?" Minett also noticed what Max Bygraves had commented on when he first worked with Howerd in 1946 – he couldn't take a compliment, and dismissed praise as unnecessary.

By this time in his life Frankie Howerd was also drinking heavily and was frequently in a bad temper – mainly with himself for not being able to remember his lines.

But the production was completed and the crew gave Frankie Howerd a round of spontaneous applause. Howerd took a microphone and said "Thank you. I've enjoyed working with all of you – except one," and off he went to his dressing room leaving everyone thinking, "All except *one*? Does he mean me?" A typical piece of Howerd mischief.

Twenty years on – and still getting the laughs

12 *Hill at the top*

There is no doubt that in his later years Benny Hill made a career out of tastelessness and vulgarity. Why he had this obsessive need to be as crude as he was is puzzling, and equally puzzling is the way that various producers allowed, even encouraged him so to be.

Possibly, through the shrewd re-editing of his material and its subsequent success in the US, he had become so profitable to Thames Television that he could do as he pleased.

Perhaps watching Benny Hill over a period of years had created an acceptance of what he peddled so that those who wanted his level of humour watched without inhibition, and those who didn't care for it just didn't watch. Certainly it seems pointless to be critical of such unimportant stuff.

On watching videos of Howerd in chat shows – such as with Russell Harty – you feel that there is a mind at work; a quirky, idiosyncratic mind but one that is alive with intelligence.

With Benny Hill in similar situations one sees charm and a "what's the harm in it" attitude, which might be shrewd and knowing and likeable, but comes over as rather negative. Men of distinction who praised him, such as Anthony Burgess and John Mortimer, saw in Hill an earthiness that to them stretched back into the mists of pre-history; and there is in mankind a desire for basic things: food, sex, and warmth. But by that yardstick there is also a need in some people for sadistic cruelty, hatred and destruction.

Would the likes of Burgess and Mortimer condone the Holocaust or the Spanish Inquisition, or, on a Benny Hill level, bullfighting or badger baiting, because the desire to hurt is also part of the human condition?

Not that I'm suggesting that Benny Hill should have been banned, but it would have been better for everyone if his many advisers and working colleagues could have persuaded him to aspire to a better sort of comedy and not just turn other people's good ideas into shabby, down-market trash.

In 1990–1, Saffron Productions (Victor Pemberton and David Spenser) made

"I'll ring head office"

"Oh! Wrong number"

an edition of the *Omnibus* series for the BBC which presented Benny Hill in the best possible light. It was beautifully directed and edited and was, in fact, an object lesson in how to make screen biographies.

In it a string of celebrities; Michael Caine, Mickey Rooney, Burt Reynolds, John Mortimer, and Walter Cronkite, the sage of US newsmen, all told how funny and entertaining Benny Hill was. There was also Charlie Chaplin's son, Eugene (who few people have ever heard of – a sort of Gummo Chaplin), who presented Benny Hill with the "Charles Chaplin Award for Comedy", in Vevey, Switzerland. In Paris, the British Ambassador threw a party to celebrate Benny's fifty years in show business, and affirmed that he and all his family were great fans of the comedian.

Benny looked very overweight and this was undoubtedly a contributing factor to his death of a heart attack shortly afterwards. It was also said at that time that he ate and drank to excess. To be honest Hill looked and sounded gross, a fact emphasised by film of his early success when, as a young man, he was undoubtedly chubby but good-looking and innocent.

In *Omnibus*, Benny, to camera, went briefly through his life story, and the shots of him in Southampton and Teddington (his last home) in shops and outside pubs gave the programme life and authority.

We also had the benefit of Richard Stone, indignant that his client had been sacked by Thames. "He was sent for like a schoolboy." Philip Jones said: "He was a perfectionist." Benny himself said, of his sacking: "I was in there for about two minutes. That was it. After all those years I'd have liked a small pat on the back." (One would have thought that more than £7,000,000 in the bank would have made up for that). And of his earlier success: "How Hill's Angels came about was through Kenny Everett's dance group, Hot Gossip. Someone said to Kenny, 'You're getting jolly good ratings', and he said, 'Thank God for Hot Gossip', and I thought – if you can't beat them join them".

Seeing early Benny Hill, both on BBC and Thames, you did catch a glimpse of how good he could be, not least in a more recent French advertisement playing different characters eating a sweetmeat.* The *Juke Box Jury* clip was trotted out and yes, it was good for its day, and John Street, who produced some BBC shows for Benny and edited the American versions of the Thames output, confessed that Benny taught him more about television comedy than anyone else. What really shone through were the clips of Benny Hill's impersonations. His W. C. Fields was excellent and his earlier Peter Lorre and Sidney Greenstreet were brilliant.

For all that I think Michael Caine summed up Benny Hill for all time when he described him as having "a face like an evil cherub."

Re-reading the Benny Hill obituaries in the posh dailies you come across two schools of thought. In one Hill is the harmless funster who by dropping his trousers let the sunlight in. The other school is more censorious saying, what many said during his lifetime, that his comedy was sexist and that, in the words of Kay Lewis in *The Guardian*:

> A small band of fanatics ... manoeuvred Benny Hill from TV despite his enduring popularity with the public.

Clearly Kay Lewis doesn't believe this and her article continues –

> A more plausible explanation has been offered by Thames – that a new
> Head of Light Entertainment, John Howard Davies noticed the show
> was slipping in the ratings and decided it was too expensive.

* Over the years Benny Hill made many successful commercials for Schweppes and Stork margarine, often appearing in the former with writer Dave Freeman.